# FANNY BRAWNE

*For my Mother and Father*

FANNY BRAWNE

From a contemporary miniature

*Photograph in the Holland Day Collection*

# FANNY BRAWNE

## *A Biography*

BY

JOANNA RICHARDSON

THE VANGUARD PRESS, INC.

PRINTED AND BOUND IN GREAT BRITAIN
BY JARROLD AND SONS LTD NORWICH

# Acknowledgments

I GLADLY record my gratitude to the numerous people who have helped me to write this biography. Mrs. Oswald Ellis has borne with all my questions about her grandmother, Fanny Brawne; and to Mr. D. H. M. D'Orsey and Miss Gertrude Hathorn I owe much of the information about the Lindon family. From Mrs. Mona M. Osborne, the grand-daughter of Charles Brown, I learned his opinion of Fanny Brawne; while Sir John Dilke searched his papers, though in vain, for unpublished material. I am indebted to Lady Ethel Dilke, who kindly allowed me to use a letter in her possession, and to Lady Unwin, who on behalf of Mr. Severn Storr, Mrs. Gerald Brooke and herself (grandchildren of Thomas Severn) gave permission to use the Joseph Severn letters they have presented to the Keats Museum. Mr. Maurice Buxton Forman has patiently answered my enquiries and allowed me, most generously, to use *Nickel List,* the *Miscellanea of Charles Brown,* and the letters written to the late Mr. H. Buxton Forman by Severn and Fanny Llanos. Mr. Edmund Blunden has given me details and read my typescript in the light of his vast knowledge of Romantic literature; Miss Dorothy Hewlett has advised me and lent me papers, and Signora Vera Cacciatore, Curator of the Keats-Shelley Memorial, has allowed me to use letters in the Rome collection. Professor Hyder Rollins has been the most magnanimous transatlantic correspondent and let me quote freely from his books, while Mr. Wilfred Samuel, Mr. Edgar Samuel and Mr. Albert M. Hyamson have enabled me to trace the Lindo genealogy, and Mr. Owen Hickey has given the typescript, like so many of my others, the benefit of his criticism.

I am also indebted to Mr. G. W. Cottrell, jr., editor of the *Harvard Library Bulletin,* for permission to print two fragmentary letters by Fanny Brawne, of which there are photographs in the Harvard Keats Memorial Collection; one of these letters appeared in the autumn *Bulletin* for 1951. Mr. William A. Jackson, director of the Harvard College Library, and Miss Mabel Steele, Custodian of the Keats Collection, have kindly allowed me to use material in their charge; while the quotations from *The Keats Circle* and *Keats and the Bostonians* are made by courtesy of the publishers, the Harvard University Press. I am most grateful to the

Oxford University Press for permission to use Mr. Forman's edition of Keats's *Letters,* the *Letters of Joseph Severn to H. Buxton Forman,* the *Miscellanea of Charles Brown* and the *Letters of Fanny Brawne to Fanny Keats*; and Messrs. John Lane, who published *The Dilke Bequest in the Hampstead Public Libraries,* have allowed me to use both text and illustrations.

Space alone prevents me from making detailed acknowledgments to the kind people whose names I now record: Richard Barnett; the Conservateur de la Bibliothèque et des Archives, Bayonne; Léon Benoliel; Mrs. Charles E. Bodurtha; A. Boudier; T. I. M. Clulow; Countess Anna Coreth; Ernest G. Crowsley; G. Garnett Ellis; A. H. Fuller; E. Giddey; F. A. Grieco; C. E. F. Hanbury Tracy; C. S. W. Harriss; Mrs. A. R. Hatley; H. K. Hudson; Dr. Kauhausen; A. Law; Miss E. D. Mercer; Sir Owen Morshead; P. H. G. Newhouse; E. F. Oppé; Professor Willard B. Pope; A. Potier; the late H. G. Potter; Albert Reinhard; J. H. RuscombeKing; Viscount St. Vincent; R. S. Scrivener; Brigadier H. C. Travell Stronge; the late Miss Gertrude M. Tuckwell; Peter Walne; F. Eliot Williams; D. R. Woodman; and the editors of *The Folkestone Herald, The Hampstead and Highgate Express* and the *Gazette de Lausanne.* I owe many details to Mr. G. F. Osborn, the archivist of the Public Libraries in the City of Westminster; the Borough Librarians of Deptford, Holborn, St. Marylebone, St. Pancras and Walthamstow; the Chief Librarians of Bermondsey, Camberwell, Croydon, Kensington and Southwark; the City Librarian of Belfast, the Directors of Municipal Libraries in Bath and Brighton, and the indefatigable staff of the Guildhall Library.

It is, however, a particular pleasure to record my debt to the Chief Librarian of Hampstead, Mr. S. J. Butcher, and to the Hampstead Public Libraries and Keats House Committee, without whose help no biography of Fanny Brawne could be written. They have allowed me to use all the unpublished material I wished, and the published letters of Fanny Brawne, and have offered me every facility in my research. Mr. J. H. Preston, the Curator of Keats House, has given me many hours of his time and shown me unfailing kindness, and the efficient staff of the Heath Branch Library satisfied my perpetual demand for literature.                                                      J. R.

# Contents

# Illustrations

## ACKNOWLEDGMENTS

*The frontispiece portrait of Fanny Brawne is reproduced by courtesy of the Dedham Historical Society, Dedham, Massachusetts, from a photograph in the Holland Day Collection of a contemporary miniature; the bust of Keats, the letters and the Bright Star Sonnet are reproduced by courtesy of the Hampstead Public Libraries and Keats House Committee, from originals in Keats House.*

# Preface

IN ALL THE shelves of Keatsian criticism and biography Fanny Brawne has been given no book to herself. It is a serious omission, because from the time Keats met her in November 1818 until his death in 1821 she was to him unquestionably the most important person. When he was introduced to her, he had already written *On First Looking into Chapman's Homer, Endymion, Isabella,* and part of *Hyperion;* in the eleven months between his meeting her and his return to Wentworth Place in October 1819, when anxiety and disease made inspiration impossible, he wrote all the other poems by which he is best known.

In many of them it would be vain to seek her influence; in others we could only suspect a mood or a passing allusion; but there still remain some of the greatest poems of Keats for which his love seems wholly and directly responsible. Without making a detailed analysis of his poetry, I hope to suggest its relation to the varying course of his betrothal.

But this is not a book of literary criticism: it is Fanny Brawne's biography, and about Fanny Brawne there has been too much speculation. Here, from the meagre facts, I have tried to reconstruct her life and exceptional character, to show, in its true proportion, her relationship to Keats, and to expose the fallacy of the Victorian legend which grew up about it. For an understanding of Fanny Brawne is vital to a full appreciation of Keats, and "as his love formed so great a part of him, we may be doing him an injustice in being silent on it." Brown's comment was wise, and Fanny Brawne herself answered: "I entirely agree with you that if his life is to be published no part ought to be kept back."

In those words, if justification be needed, she explains and sanctions this book.

J. R.

## NOTE

*Numbers occurring in the text relate to relevant notes printed at the end of the book and grouped under the main section titles. Asterisks refer the reader to Appendix I, which gives further details about friends and acquaintances of Fanny Brawne who feature in the text.*

# Prologue

## I

✦✦✦

"HAMPSTEAD," wrote an inhabitant in the eighteenth century, "is a most delightful village, very happy in its Situation, being somewhat romantick yet every way pleasant. It is situated upon several little Hills, on a high ground of different Soils; some Parts being upon a Clay Loom and other Parts on a Gravel. Here it is, that you draw in a pure and balmy Air, with the Heavens clear and serene above you, in that Season of the Year that the great and populous City of *London* (from which it is distant not above four miles) is cover'd with Fogs, Smoaks, and other thick Darkness, being," he added, "frequently oblig'd to burn Candles in the middle of the Day."

From their pleasant eminence, higher than the new dome of St. Paul's, the villagers of Hampstead looked down on the panorama of London. Not for them "the noisome Smell of stinking Fogs, or other malignant Fumes and Vapours," which, as they pointed out, were "too, too common in large Cities." On the slopes of their several little hills they stood, "bless'd with the benign and comfortable rays of a glorious Sun, breathing a free and wholesome Air" and admiring the exten⁄sive view; and Dr. John Soame, inviting visitors to the wells, would take them to the summit of the Heath to gaze over "nine or ten counties at least," to divert themselves with the sight of ships upon the Thames and the view of several fine palaces to be seen with the naked eye.

The wells were passing out of fashion by the turn of the century. The Heath itself was grander than it is today and wealthier in wild birds and rare, unlooked-for flowers, and a single road, now known as Haverstock Hill, joined the metropolis to this hill-top, Morland village. A devious downhill path led through the country fields to the Brawnes' farm in the hamlet of West End.

It was here, on a summer Saturday, August 9th, 1800, when the corn harvest had begun in most counties and the crops had never been more abundant, that Samuel Brawne's first child, a brown-haired girl, was born. He decided to call her Frances after her mother.

## II

❖❖❖

FANNY BRAWNE did not enter an undistinguished family. Sir John de Brawne had come over at the Conquest, John Brawne had been Abbot of Abingdon in the days of Henry VIII, while the Brawne family of London and Saintbury in the County of Warwick had been noted in the time of the Stuarts, and Sir Hugh Brawne, a citizen and vintner of London, had died possessed of estates in several counties. Four of Fanny's aunts, Ann and Jane, Mary and Margaret, bore the same names as the children of the knight. Fanny's grandfather, Samuel Brawne, a coachmaster and stable-keeper, had married Jane Richardson, said to be the descendant of a Lord Chief Justice, and he had shown in his material achievements a little of the energy of his forebears: he had owned a cottage at Twyford and the Coach and Horses Inn, Castle Street, off the Strand, the starting-point for frequent coaches to Hammersmith and Clapham; and shortly before his death he had moved to a farm in Kilburn, which was both an impressive agricultural venture and a large and visible proof of his commercial success. Wise and progressive, he had provided for apprenticeship fees should his daughters decide to learn trades. After his death in the summer of 1787 Jane Brawne, some of her daughters, and her nine-year-old son, Samuel Vernon, had continued to live at Kilburn. Occasionally the boy's Brummell cousins, William, George and Maria, would arrive from St. James's. They were the children of Mrs. Brawne's sister, who had married William Brummell, private secretary of Lord North, and George gained a certain significance as Beau Brummell.[1]

These were the paternal ancestors and relations of Fanny Brawne, from whom, perhaps, she inherited her strong common sense, determination, and her love of life. Her mother was Frances Ricketts, "a lady of West Indian connexions and some little fortune."* The Ricketts family in the West Indies at the end of the eighteenth century had been administrators of distinction: one had served for many years as Attorney-General and Advocate-General of Jamaica, and another as a member of the island's council, while a third, George Poyntz Ricketts, "a very superior character," had been Captain-General and Governor-in-Chief of Tobago and later of Barbados. More-over, as *The Gentleman's Magazine* discreetly suggested, the family did not lack respectable relations. Governor Ricketts was himself a cousin of the Earl of Liverpool, and William Henry, of the Jamaican council, was the brother-in-law of Nelson's commander, St. Vincent, while his son was named as the heir to the viscounty. Nor was financial distinction lacking, for John Ricketts,* the maternal grandfather of Fanny Brawne, had amassed estates in Kent and throughout the City of London.

A man of strong business sense, however, John Ricketts retained inflexible puritan principles and an exclusive appre-ciation of business sense in others. His son John* became a City cheesemonger and duly prospered; his daughter Mary* married a man of financial ability, and Margaret* married a steady calico printer. Of Frances's future husband, Samuel Brawne,* who was twenty-one and had no commercial reputation, John Ricketts could not bring himself to approve.

It was thus in the absence of the bride's father, in the bride-groom's parish church, that on November 13th, 1799, Samuel Brawne married Frances Ricketts. But there could have been no more fitting place than Hampstead for the ceremony, and we must admire the prescience of *The Gentleman's Magazine* which, among the Marriages of Remarkable Persons recorded for November, promptly included "Mr. Samuel Brawne, of West End, to Miss Ricketts, of Surrey-place, Kent road."


## III

❖❖❖

FANNY WAS christened in Hampstead on November 1st, 1800. The Brawnes were still living in West End, and here their second daughter, Jane,* was born four days before Christmas 1802. She died at Ealing in the following August. Why the Brawnes were in Ealing must remain surmise, for Samuel still held property in West End and his mother in Kilburn; but in Ealing they remained for at least thirteen months, and their first son, Samuel,* was born there on July 26th, 1804. By the beginning of 1807 they had returned to Hampstead.

Fanny Brawne, as a small girl, was not unlike Maria Brum-mell in the Gainsborough portrait; she had the same brown hair, intensely blue eyes, and the same precocious expression. But her precocity lay deeper: the consequence, perhaps, of being the eldest in a fast-increasing family. It was not merely a youthful imitation of adult behaviour: she needed to be pur-poseful; and later this strength of mind became one of her obvious merits. Another virtue, if the word is not too large for a child, was her affectionate nature; indeed, on one occasion she was "delicately reproved" for spoiling her younger brother.[2] They were walking on Hampstead Heath with a friend when, in the distance, a soldier fell off his horse; Fanny promptly covered Samuel's face with her shawl. "Why did you do that?"

KEATS

From the bust by Patrick MacDowell

HERBERT  BRAWNE-LINDON

From a photograph taken in early middle age

asked the friend, "The boy was in no danger; he was too
far off." "But if Samuel had seen him," Fanny answered, "he
would have cried for him, and then he must have had him,
and however should we have got the soldier home?"

If the younger children received both parental and sisterly
attention, there is no doubt that Fanny herself, being the
Brawnes' first child, intelligent and abounding in gaiety, was
indulged by both her parents. Mrs. Brawne, well-meaning and
warm-hearted, might be summed in the word "motherly,"
while Mr. Brawne was, it seems, a fond and tolerant father.
"It is people of this disposition," as Fanny commented years
later, "that invariably spoil their children and bring them up
such plagues as no doubt I was." Her impatient demand for
stories was sometimes satisfied when her father told her of her
great-uncle, Joseph Vernon,* who had given him his name and
had acted at Drury Lane half a century before with David
Garrick. Joseph Vernon had distinguished himself in comedy,
his wife had taken part in light opera; and if Fanny took after
the Brummells when she acted stylishly, it was partly due to
her great-aunt and -uncle that she deeply enjoyed the theatre,
showed a strong predilection for comedy, and was herself
called, with some justice, Millamant. As a child she enlarged
the tales she heard and more which she invented, with boundless imagination, borrowing her mother's clothes for a fantastic
game, playing in the barns at West End and round the half-
buried masonry which remained from Kilburn Priory. She
delighted in the grotesque, as children do, the dramatic and the
bright, spinning stories round the coaches at the Old Bell Inn,
Dick Turpin's gallop through Hampstead, the ghost at the
Spaniards' Tavern, and the characters who, she was told,
attended the notorious fair at West End. She was fond of
animals and wandered round the farm, feeding birds and
adopting favourite kittens, and often she roamed with her
father on the wide and inviting Heath. In 1807 her younger

brother, John,* was born; he died in infancy, but the memory of a little girl is short, and in April 1809, a few months after his death, she was consoled by the birth of her sister, Margaret.* Within the next year the Brawnes moved to Kentish Town; they may well have stayed for a time with Mrs. Brawne's brother, for a certain John Ricketts lived at The Grove.

The hamlet of Kentish Town, at about this time, consisted of a long street going up towards Highgate, and chiefly com-posed of hunting-boxes and lodging-houses for the inhabitants of London. The visitor approaching from the City would see a small house on the outskirts inscribed: "This house begins the entrance of Kentish Town"; and where the road met the Hampstead road he would find a dairy, with benches outside, where unlimited milk, fresh from the cow, was provided for all who came. Those who preferred stronger drink would go to the Assembly Rooms which had been described as the provincial Almack's. The building was seen on its gala nights "all radiant with light, reflecting its brilliancy down the entire road," and the proprietor still offered a choice assortment of wines, spirits and liquors, "all of which he was *determined* to sell on the most *valuable* terms." There were a skittle-ground, summer-house and garden, "and every other accommodation for the convenience of those who might think proper to *make an excursion* during the summer months. A good ordinary on Sundays at two o'clock." To furnished lodgings in Kentish Town, during these summer months, came those afflicted with consumption and other disorders, while City sportsmen could be seen coursing over the fields.

Fanny Brawne, as a child of nine, would have watched the horses being shod in the smithy at the foot of West Hill, and admired the deer across the road as they browsed on the lawns of the big estate known as Bateman's Folly; she would have heard how Queen Elizabeth went hunting and hawking at Kentish Town and how her palace became the country house

of Nell Gwynne, and how some of the first ascents by balloon
had been made from Kentish Town fields. On particular
occasions Mrs. Brawne would take the children to Walworth,
to visit her father, John Ricketts, who was living in Richmond
Place, and sometimes they stayed with him in Margate; for him,
we know, Fanny felt a special affection, and it must have been
one of her first remembered griefs when he died in the autumn
of 1809. He bequeathed considerable estates in Deptford, West
Smithfield and elsewhere, on trust to Mrs. Brawne, as if she
were independent of her husband; after her death it was to
remain on trust for her children. John Ricketts left a vast
amount of property; and it is all the more unpleasant to read
that as Samuel Brawne had owed him some £200 and arrears
of interest since 1801, the trustees were to retain £50 a year out
of Frances's legacy until the debt was fully paid.*

In the spring of 1810 a deeper sorrow ended the Brawnes'
domestic happiness. Their removal to Kentish Town may well
have been influenced by the hamlet's fame among consump-
tives and other invalids. Fanny, who suffered from asthma,
was small and pale. Tuberculosis was widespread in the early
nineteenth century: Mrs. Brawne's sister, Lucy,* had died of a
decline, and the young Samuel Brawne may have been consumptive already. It seems that Mr. Brawne had reached the
last stages of consumption and felt that death was imminent,
for on April 11th, 1810, though he was but thirty-five, he made
his will;* within a few days he had died, and on April 21st
he was buried at St. Martin-in-the-Fields.

## IV

→◆←

MRS. BRAWNE was left a widow, with three young children,
at the age of thirty-nine. It seems likely that she lived some time
longer in Kentish Town; and in 1812 Samuel Brawne was in

Brompton, probably at school. The children's aunt, Elizabeth Baker, invited them to Croydon and later to Ashurst in Kent, and sometimes they stayed with their uncle, John Ricketts, in Stoke Newington.

During these years Fanny herself was at school; her mother may already have taught her some elementary French, but now she learned to read it fluently and to translate from German. The engravings in her scrapbook of Sir Thomas More and the Duke of Buckingham may suggest some early interest in history, while her knowledge of historical costume always impressed her friends. She had long since been taught to sew, but now she began fine embroidery. She learned to dance the quadrille, and as she was musical and graceful she danced well; and in deportment, which stood high on the curriculum, she excelled: "Dress, manner and carriage," she came to write, were what one acquaintance needed: "A person must be a great beauty to look well without them, but they are certainly within the reach of anybody of understanding." It was at school that she began to appreciate Hogarth and Dürer, and enjoyed Stothard's illustrations to *Robinson Crusoe*; while in literature she started to form her independent tastes. "I am," she said later, "by no means a great poetry reader—and like few things *not* comic out of Shakespeare. Comedy of all sorts pleases me." One of her school-friends gave her the serious poems of Byron and she went "half wild about them learning and repeating continually when alone"; but as Fanny's friendship dwindled to mere acquaintance and she came to see poetry in perspective, Byron's work soon lost its value and the book was given away. But "one thing is certain to me," she remarked on the same occasion, "which is, that it is impossible to *write* about books, for before you can get out your sensations about one line the letter is finished."

One of her most treasured books, at least in her early years, must have been a small volume published about 1780 at the reasonable price of a shilling "or 1s. 6d., neatly bound"; this was *The New London and Country Songster; or, a Banquet of Vocal Music*. This compendious publication, we are told, included "some of the *best* and *most favourite* Scotch, Irish and Welch Songs, *now in Vogue*. Together with *a Variety* of Country dances, &c., and *A Curious Collection* of Original Toasts, Sentiments, and Hobnobs *at this Time used* in the most polite circles. The Whole Being Brought down to the *present year* by Mr. VERNON." There followed many songs which had been sung by Fanny's great-uncle at Vauxhall, and perhaps with her younger brother she tried the country dances described at the end of the book; it would have been pleasant to see her work out the steps of *Miss Hobart's Fancy* or attempt *The Rural Assembly* and *Admiral Rodney's Triumph*.

Fanny's uncle, John Ricketts, died in April 1816. He left £1,100 to his three sisters and £1,500 on trust for the three Brawne children;* until they came of age it was to remain an investment, the dividends to be paid to Mrs. Brawne for their maintenance and education, and the trustees were directed to pay up to £200 for Samuel's business training. John Ricketts had always been particularly friendly to the Brawnes, and his affection had been returned, for among the bequests to Samuel was "the Silver Tankard given me by his late Father." The remainder of John Ricketts' plate was divided between his sisters, and the property which had not been specified was sold for Mrs. Brawne's benefit: perhaps he had already contributed to her children's education, for she seems to have been the least affluent of his sisters. However that may be, his will was promptly proved and in the spring of 1816 the Brawnes looked forward to a steadier future. Nothing further is known of them until 1818, when they took Charles Brown's* house in Hampstead for the summer.

# V

✦✦✦

GERARD, compiling his *Herbal*, studied the flowers of Hampstead, and Linnaeus knelt to thank God for the glory of the
Heath; and in the nineteenth century, when Mrs. Siddons knew
it, and Scott and Wordsworth, Lamb and Coleridge, Blake
and Constable wandered on its hills and Shelley sailed paper
boats on a Hampstead pond to amuse the son of Leigh Hunt,
the Heath kept its votaries.

The ancient Middlesex forest had once covered Hampstead
hill, and beeches of immense growth lingered in the confines of
Ken Wood, where lilies of the valley had been known to grow
abundantly; white and yellow water-lilies hid the ponds in
summer, while on the west Heath the harebells and dog-roses,
the pale-blue, purple-streaked marsh violets, the wild pear, crab-
apple and wild bullace trees would flourish in their season.
Wood crowfoot, scattered in the west and east, again suggested
the bounds of the old dense forest of deciduous growth; barberry
and dewberry, bramble and wild raspberry, speedwell, peri-
winkle and wild hyacinth would all take root, the greater
celandine and opium poppy grew on the old brickfields, while
enchanter's nightshade flourished in damp places where plants
used for incantations are found. By the holly trees near the new
Spaniards' Road the nightingales were heard, and kestrels flew
observantly above the cornfields.

In the harvest season, haymakers from the Fens would come
down for casual labour, and in fine weather the gipsies camped
near the willow plantations. A host of local washerwomen, who
had lived longer than memory in shacks on the Heath, washed
Hampstead's laundry and spread it out on the hills round the
Vale of Health; the donkey-drivers took their stand on the
Heath wherever they chose, and speculative lace-makers in
their short red cloaks, frilled with black lace, and black bonnets,

carrying cushions with varicoloured bobbins swinging from them, would sell thread lace to chance customers and take orders from others. Foreign-looking women, from Holland or the Savoy, peddled their miniature brooms of poplar wood and cried: "Buy a broom, buy a broom! A large one for a lady, a small one for a baby! Buy a broom, buy a broom!" In the wilder parts of Hampstead, by the long foot-path from London which went through the Conduit Fields, no one went by night, and Cut-throat Alley, which crossed the grounds of Belsize House, was hardly used even by day.

Wentworth Place, in the Lower Heath Quarter, was a block of two houses, white-stuccoed and semi-detached, built three years before by Charles Brown and Charles Wentworth Dilke. Brown's house was smaller than the other, for he was a bachelor while Dilke was a married man with a family. The friends shared the garden and its abundant fruit and vegetables. Wentworth Place was designed for convenience; it stood in a lane near the public pond on South End Green, and not far from Picketts' Dairy, the best-kept in the parish, while the coach stopped only a few yards away. In 1818, as the Brawnes arrived for the summer, the roadmakers were completing Downshire Hill at the top of the lane, and where the two roads met, the builders were erecting St. John's Chapel because the parish church had grown too small for local needs.

The popularity of Hampstead was indeed increasing: the number of its inhabitants had risen from four to five thousand even in Fanny's lifetime, and people who no longer came to drink the chalybeate waters and found that "the Wells' Ball-room, instead of being appropriated to the votaries of dancing, had wholly changed its occupation and was now a chapel," would repair instead to "the present very elegant assembly-rooms" on Holly Bush Hill, with card rooms and supper rooms adjoining; the assembly rooms had been partly built out of Romney's studio, and could only be reached, for a time, through the garden and kitchen of the Holly Bush Tavern, whose landlord, Thomas Lovelock, supplied refreshments; and here, until the latter part of the century, all Hampstead came for concerts, lectures, conversaziones, public meetings, and to dance at the public balls.

Society was varied and attractive; young officers from the Peninsular Wars, perhaps from Waterloo, rode over for the balls from the barracks in St. John's Wood, while exotic French and Spanish *émigrés* came from their lodgings round Oriel House in Church Row and the chapel in Holly Place; and to this society, not long after she left school, Fanny Brawne was introduced. Her closest friend was Mrs. Rodd,* the wife of the surgeon in the High Street, and the Rodds later introduced her to Mr. Elley, who lived at the end of Well Walk; in his large house and spacious grounds he entertained in the grand manner. It was through the Rodds that Fanny heard about Baron Dimsdale, and probably met him. He lived in Pond Street and asked the doctor to call three or four times a week, not so much for his health's sake, but because he liked a chat and Dr. Rodd had travelled widely. The Baron would describe his father's journey to Russia to inoculate the Empress Catherine for smallpox; the Empress had tactfully provided the elder Dimsdale with a passport and told him to escape at once if he thought she was likely to die; but so successful had the operation been that the Dimsdales were now barons of the Russian Empire, and among their treasures were miniatures of the Empress and her son, and a gold snuff-box richly set with diamonds, a present from the Grand Duke. To all this Fanny, who wanted to travel, would listen delightedly.

At the Davenports',* at 2, Church Row, the dullness of the host was more than compensated; for his elder daughter, Margaret, was "rather a genteel girl" and innumerable members of the French and Spanish colonies would come for cards and quadrilles. "Don't suppose it was a grand party," wrote Fanny once, "there could not be above forty people and their rooms are small, but it was a very pleasant one." The house, which has been unpardonably demolished, was one of the two finest Georgian buildings in Hampstead; imposing pillars, topped by stone pineapples, stood on either side of the gate, and a flagged path led up the small garden to a finely moulded door, while someone who entered the house at the end of the century remembers that it was panelled throughout and still had the original fire-places.

In these surroundings Fanny moved as soon as she entered society; but within a few weeks of taking Brown's half of Wentworth Place the Brawnes had established the firmest friendship with Dilke and his wife next door. Maria Dilke, the daughter of a north-country yeoman, combined the steadiness of her Yorkshire family with a vivacity of her own; and her physical inability to be punctual was, like her unrecorded faults, forgiven her because she was kind-hearted and remark-ably pretty. Long before she came of age she had married Dilke, who worked at the Navy Pay Office, Somerset House, and was not at the time nineteen. He had since made some mark in literature by editing *Old English Plays*, and proved himself a man of integrity and strong opinions, while his affection for his wife was only equalled, if indeed it was not exceeded, by his blind devotion to their only son. Charley, born in 1810, was the constant companion, and nearly the contemporary, of the nine-year-old Margaret Brawne. Between Mrs. Brawne and the kindly, energetic Mrs. Dilke there was much in common.

In these sunlit summer days, Hampstead looked inviting. Philips, the old gardener, would bring in daily baskets of fruit; the Heath was green with ferns, empurpled with heather, while the buttercups gave the sun gold for gold. The Brawnes had not lost their affection for Hampstead, and now they were bound to the village by a new friendship. As their tenancy drew to an end at Wentworth Place, Mrs. Brawne took a lease of Elm Cottage, which stood on the corner of Red Lion Hill and Downshire Hill.

## VI

❖❖❖

MRS. KEATS, a vivacious and intelligent woman, had shown "doting fondness" for John, her eldest son, whose every fancy (and he had many) she indulged. He returned her affection warmly, and when, in his fifteenth year, she died of consumption, his long and impassioned grief had been painful to witness. Perhaps his mother's death increased his devotion to his small sister, Fanny, the youngest of the family, but at the time she was only six and hardly a companion; and of the women in his immediate circle there remained only his grandmother, Mrs. Jennings. Since his ninth year, when his mother had remarried, Keats had spent his school holidays with Mrs. Jennings in Edmonton, as his younger brothers, George and Tom, came to do; while Fanny, who did not yet go to school, lived all the time at her grandmother's. To the four children Mrs. Jennings showed all her dependable north-country kindness, and Keats's first known poem was written on her death. This new bereavement, soon after his nineteenth birthday, deprived him of her almost maternal care and of the growing companionship of his sister. Fanny was sent to school in Walthamstow by Richard Abbey, her guardian, and later she became a member of his household; Abbey was remarkably stubborn and obtuse and it was not often that he let Keats see her again.

The absence of women from his family helped to embarrass Keats when he met them elsewhere: it was generally through George, who never lacked assurance, that he met them at all. This embarrassment may be seen in some of his early poems which are written in the style of a coy votary: Georgiana Wylie would not have recognized in the "twin water-lillies" and "those beauties scarce discerned" a description of her feet; and Keats's three sonnets *To Woman* show the clumsy and somewhat conventional fervour of his worship. He burned to be a Calidore, "a very Red Cross Knight—a stout Leander," to enjoy a love like those he found in legend and romance; yet in *Calidore*, as in the sonnets, he shows too plainly by his awkward courtesies that he is only an "aspiring boy." Both in his poetry and in his letters he also shows his constant sense of physical inferiority. Keats's head was that of a Greek god, his body compact and well proportioned, but he was only five feet tall, and "I being somewhat stunted," he wrote, "am taken for nothing," and "after all I do think better of Womankind than to suppose they care whether Mister John Keats five feet high likes them or not." One of his sonnets, addressed to an unknown woman, begins with the words: "Had I a man's fair form," and describing the grandeur of the Lake District he makes the poignant remark: "I never forgot my stature so completely." The very assurance of admiration would hurt him, he was so convinced of his physical unworthiness; and to Keats, who rejoiced intensely in all forms of beauty, the consciousness, whether right or wrong, of his own imperfect appearance mattered much.

But he had not found imperfection in himself alone; since boyhood he had never known a woman who reconciled his ideal with reality or satisfied his "yearning Passion for the beautiful." *Endymion* is the record of a quest which was made most ardently, and long in vain, by Keats himself.

There were several women for whom he felt a passing fancy: Mary Frogley, the cousin of his friend Richard Woodhouse, was known, it seems, to the Keats brothers at least as early as 1816, and William Howitt described her as the poet's "old flame." "Many of his verses," Howitt wrote in 1838, "were addressed to her; and a very lovely young woman she was, I doubt not. She sent us the other day three sketches of him to look at." But Mary Frogley probably had the sketches from her cousin who had acquired them from Severn or Charles Brown; and though she possessed five poems written in Keats's hand, the fact that these included a valentine *To Emma* suggests that she was his literary critic rather than his muse. Emma herself may have been related to George Felton Mathew, Keats's friend, and in one of Mathew's cousins, Ann or Caroline, perhaps in both of them, Keats showed an interest; yet again it was transient and superficial. "Tell Haydon," he wrote to his brothers in 1817, "to Kiss his Hand at Betty over the Way for me yea and to spy at her for me . . . give my Love to the Miss Reynoldses . . . write to me soon about them all." The identity of the mildly attractive Betty has not yet been discovered, but whatever Jane and Mariane Reynolds felt about Keats, his affection for them was consistently platonic; and though he addressed the letters to Jane and teased her a little "for Love," the correspondence, effervescent and gay, was intended for both sisters, and the tone remained that of an elder brother. For Mrs. Leigh Hunt, it seems, he felt little affection: she was merely an interruption to her husband's company; while Elizabeth Kent, her unmarried sister and a well-known botanist, might have found herself with dismay among the "set of Devils, whom I detest . . . a set of Women, who . . . set themselves up for towers of Babel in Languages Sapphos in Poetry—Euclids in Geo-metry—and everything in nothing. . . . I had longed," wrote Keats, "for some real feminine Modesty in these things."

He was disillusioned, often indifferent, sometimes sharply critical; he had not even touched the common level of love, let alone the depth of passion which he demanded. He was twenty-two, and physical experience could hardly have been unknown to him; but the power of romance and spiritual love remained unfelt.

From this barren dream, in which he had lived since he had become aware of his poetic ideal and of his own virility, Keats was awakened in the early summer of 1818, when his brother

George, about to emigrate to America, married Georgiana Augusta Wylie. Keats had been "very fond of her" for some time, but he could not allow himself to love his sister-in-law with the boundless fervour which he would show to his own chosen wife; he did not feel, perhaps, that she was physically beautiful, nor did Georgiana realize the poetic dream of Keats immediately and wholly. Yet this imaginative girl of sixteen he "delighted to honour": she brought a new, refreshing gaiety into his life, she was unspoiled, carefree and unselfish, "the most disinterrested woman" whom Keats had known. She it was who first showed him that happiness was entirely real and could be found in marriage; and in an "unearthly, spiritual and etherial temper of mind" he always loved her.

On June 22nd, 1818, George and his wife left London on the first stage of their journey to America; they were accompanied by Keats and Brown who were beginning their tour of the Lake District and Scotland, and at Liverpool the brothers parted. There came then, upon Keats, the full force of his new emotion. Throughout the Scottish tour, increasingly, he felt his spiritual ferment: "Who would not like to discover over again that Cleopatra was a Gipsey, Helen a Rogue and Ruth a deep one?" It was an echo of Mercutio. "I have spoken to you against Marriage," he told Reynolds a few days later, "but it was general. the Prospect in those matters has been to me so blank, that I have not been unwilling to die—I would not now, for I have inducements to Life—I must see my little Nephews in America, and I must see you marry your lovely Wife . . . believe me I have more than once yearne'd for the time of your happiness to come, as much as I could for myself after the lips of Juliet." But now he did not only wish for the happiness of others; he had felt the pleasure of loving Georgiana, and he had not thought it possible to become so devoted in so short a time. "Things like these, and they are real, have made me resolve to have a care of my health." How far had Keats progressed since

March when he had written of "things semi-real such as Love
. . . which require a greeting of the Spirit to make them wholly
exist"!

But Georgiana, who had wrought this spiritual change,
remained in his memory alone, and actuality, too, had prompted
his confession: coming down to Ballantrae, just before he wrote
to Reynolds, he had met a wedding party, and the sight had
touched his innermost mind, even to poetry. Increasingly,
Keats needed marriage: there only remained the apparently
irreconcilable difference between the young ideal to which he
clung and the reality of the Reynolds sisters. He decided to pay
them no more visits: "I am certain I have not a right feeling
towards Women—at this moment I am striving to be just to
them but I cannot—Is it because they fall so far beneath my
Boyish imagination? When I was a Schoolboy I thought a fair
Woman a pure Goddess, my mind was a soft nest in which
some one of them slept, though she knew it not—I have no
right to expect more than their reality. I thought them etherial
above Men—I find them perhaps equal. . . . Insult may be
inflicted in more ways than by Word or action. . . . I do not
like to think insults in a Lady's Company. . . . When I am
among Women I have evil thoughts, malice spleen—I cannot
speak or be silent—I am full of Suspicions and therefore listen
to nothing—I am in a hurry to be gone—You must be chari-
table and put all this down to my being disappointed since
Boyhood . . . I must absolutely get over this—but how? The
only way is to find the root of evil, and so cure it 'with backward
mutters of dissevering Power'—that is a difficult thing. . . ."
Whether he had meditated alone, or discussed the problem with
Brown, or had had some disappointing sexual experience, we
do not know, but he told Tom soon afterwards: "With respect
to Women I think I shall be able to conquer my passions here-
after better than I have yet done." On August 18th, disturbed
in mind, and suffering too much from an ulcerated throat to

continue his tour, he was back in Hampstead. He found Tom
pathetically weak and ill.

In August and September, while his own "little Indisposi⁄
tion" continued, and Tom's consumption grew steadily and
rapidly worse, there appeared the libellous *Blackwood* and
*Quarterly* articles. Their effect upon Keats, though it never
reached the dimensions drawn by his early biographers, was
severe at a time of prolonged depression and strain.

But even before the *Quarterly* article was published, a more
powerful and subtle influence had found its way into Keats's
mind. Jane Reynolds had suggested coming to see Tom, and
Keats was touched by her kindness; he broke his resolution,
visited the sisters, and on the first day he called he met their
cousin, Jane Cox. He found, ironically, in Jane Reynolds's
cousin, the first woman who strongly attracted him. "She is not
a Cleopatra, but she is at least a Charmian. She has a rich east⁄
ern look; she has fine eyes and fine manners. When she comes
into a room she makes an impression the same as the Beauty of
a Leopardess. She is too fine and too con[s]cious of herself to
repulse any Man who may address her—from habit she thinks
that nothing *particular*. I always find myself more at ease with
such a woman; the picture before me always gives me a life and
animation which I cannot possibly feel with anything inferior
—I am at such times too much occupied in admiring to be
awkward or in a tremble. I forget myself entirely because I live
in her."

Keats had been unself⁄conscious in the presence of Georgiana;
but not until he met Jane Cox did he record that he was lost in
admiration. His sense of physical inferiority had gone, and with
it, suddenly, his mental unrest: and as he had felt spiritual love
for Georgiana, so he now felt its complement for Charmian.
He was irresistibly, and, he thought, dangerously drawn to her,
and it was with some satisfaction that he sent Dilke a line from
Ronsard and the comment: "You have passed your Romance

and I never gave into it." But in a letter to Reynolds, to whom he sent more of the sonnet, he revealed the deeper part of his mind and the difficulty of his struggle: "I never was in love— yet the voice and the shape of a Woman has haunted me these two days—at such a time when the relief, the feverous relief of Poetry seems a much less crime—This morning Poetry has conquered ... I feel escaped from a new strange and threatening sorrow.—and I am thankful for it. There is an awful warmth about my heart like a load of Immortality." His dying brother, Charmian and poetry had rung changes in his mind.

In mid-October, within a month of meeting Charmian, and when he needed sympathy, Keats met a woman whom he had known at Hastings and seen again on a visit to the English Opera. She was possibly the friend of Taylor and Reynolds, the beautiful Mrs. Isabella Jones[3] at whose suggestion, it is said, he wrote the *Eve of St. Agnes*; and the artistic surroundings in which she lived, her intellectual companionship, and the curious fact that he continued to visit her for some months, suggest that she might be the Mrs. Jones to whom some of his books were given. Her behaviour seemed strange; she had known George and Reynolds, but she wanted her friendship with him to be hidden from acquaintances. For his part, he expected to see her occasionally, and was content to know her for her mind and friendship alone.

Within the last four months Keats had experienced the attractions of spirit, body and intellect: but he had felt them separately and none in all intensity, nor had he yet found his poetic ideal. The presence of Tom, who was by now critically ill, made the thought of marriage seem unforgivable. On his twenty-third birthday, the last day of October, Keats recorded his hope that he would never marry: "The roaring of the wind is my wife and the Stars through the window pane are my Children. The mighty abstract Idea of Beauty I have in all things stifles the more divided and minute domestic happiness

—an amiable wife and sweet Children I contemplate as part of that Beauty—but I must have a thousand of those beautiful particles to fill up my heart . . . I should be most enviable—with the yearning Passion I have for the beautiful, connected and made one with the ambition of my intellect."

Within a few days of writing this, Keats met Fanny Brawne, and the first week that he knew her he became her vassal.

# Keats and Fanny Brawne
## *1818-1821*

### I
♦♦♦

FANNY BRAWNE was now eighteen. She was "beautiful and elegant, graceful, silly, fashionable and strange."

She was small, her eyes were blue and often enhanced by blue ribbons in her brown hair; her mouth expressed deter‑ mination and a sense of humour and her smile was disarming. She was not conventionally beautiful: her nose was a little too aquiline, her face too pale and thin (some called it sallow). But she knew the value of elegance; velvet hats and muslin bonnets, crêpe hats with argus feathers, straw hats embellished with grapes and tartan ribbons: Fanny noticed them all as they came from Paris. She could answer, at a moment's notice, any ques‑ tion on historical costume. She collected prints of cashmere dresses, tulle mantillas embroidered with flowers, tunics of Smyrna silk and muslin gowns, and no one knew better than she did the relative merits of satin and crêpe lisse, or decided more firmly that "the bands of course will be put in with small cords covered with muslin . . . I think net sleeves out of the question." She followed the fashions with pleasure if without economy, for "I really think over economy the most expensive thing there is."

The Brawnes possessed a piano and Fanny enjoyed music; her voice was "singularly sweet."[1] She was fond of dancing and moved with natural but cultivated grace. If she were ever "silly" it was only because she took some momentary youthful pose, for in fact she understood people with an insight beyond

22

her age. She was tolerant, but not of insincerity; she was kind
but she held firm opinions, her mind was clear, her sense of
purpose strong, she could be diplomatic or disconcertingly
candid. She was an eager politician, fiery in discussion; she was
a voluminous reader, finding pleasure in *Frankenstein* or the
works of Lamb, a "trumpery novel" or a two-volume history
of literature. Her book list[2] included the *Memoirs* of Evelyn,
the *Memoirs of the Court of Elizabeth*, Lord Orford's *Reminiscences* and the *Tales of My Landlord*. We may feel the influence
of Keats in her choice of Hazlitt's *Lectures on the English Poets*,
and perhaps, as the author of *Isabella* and the lover of Chaucer,
he had recommended "Drydens poems from Boccacio and
Chaucer—6s." Indeed, books were her favourite topic of conversation: "there is nothing I like better to talk about unless it is
to such a very great judge that I am affraid they will think all my
delightful criticism nonsense"; and if her list of serious books
shows her discrimination, her comment proves that she was
modest.

Such was Fanny Brawne, whose sayings were quoted in
Hampstead; "people used to repeat her latest *bons mots*."[3] "She
was most animated," Gerald Griffin wrote, "lively and even
witty in conversation. She quite dazzled me."

## II

FANNY BRAWNE first met Keats at the Dilkes', at Wentworth
Place, in November 1818. His eager, Grecian face must have
fulfilled all the descriptions which Mrs. Dilke had given her,
and her own conception of a poet. As Mrs. Dilke had
said, he was unconventional: his collar overlapped his lapels,
his cravat was carelessly tied, his coat was bright; and as
Mrs. Dilke had led her to expect, he was generous in mind
and brilliant in conversation.

She thought enough about him to lose her assurance when they met again: she pretended not to like him. Occasionally she had "a chat and a tiff" with him, sometimes she forgot her poise and said outrageous things, once he gave her a reprimand for her language; but she listened to him with heartfelt admira/ tion, and his conversation, serious, gentle, punning or discur/ sive, she found interesting "in the highest degree." She told him how her great/uncle had acted with Mrs. Robinson in *The Winter's Tale*; he told her that his greatest ambition was to write plays, he spoke of Shakespeare eagerly, of his own dramatic criticism and of Brown's free admission for life to Drury Lane. He offered to lend her his copy of Molière;[4] they spoke of French literature. Hazlitt, he thought, had criticized Voltaire and Rabelais with fine discrimination; Fanny deter/ mined to read Hazlitt's lectures. When Keats made puns she delighted in his wit, and when he became nonsensical she "adored him for his humour."[5] She had heard from the Dilkes of the malevolent articles on his poetry, but nothing in his animated behaviour told her that he was "brooding over any secret grief or disappointment."[6] Only when he remembered Tom did he grow anxious and dejected; but Fanny could sympathize because she, too, had a delicate younger brother and sufficient remembrance of her father's death. Mrs. Brawne began to ask Keats to Elm Cottage, and as he had no mother she showed him maternal solicitude. He thought her "a very nice woman," for she was fulfilling a need he had felt since Mrs. Jennings died.

Throughout November, though he tried to ease his mind in writing *Hyperion*, he suffered from his vigil at Tom's side, his want to confide and his duty to guard his brother from anxiety. Early on the first day of December Tom died. Some years before, Keats had written that his love for his brothers was "an affection 'passing the Love of Women' . . . the thought of them has always stifled the impression that any woman might otherwise have made upon me." In his daily life that profound and steady love was no longer possible.

Fanny showed him the depth of her understanding. She gave him invigorating sympathy, keeping his mind from the past and from introspection; she encouraged his love of life by her obvious interest in him, and by her vivacity. Remarkably soon his own gaiety returned.

She had always chosen her dresses cleverly and she wore them well. Her elegance was not easily acquired, for she needed to curl her abundant hair every night.[7] But her care was appreciated; for when in mid-December she had a friend to stay, and called her a paragon of fashion, and told Keats that she would willingly change places with Caroline Robinson,* he wrote in his indignation: "What a Stupe—[Miss Brawne] is superior as a Rose to a Dandelion." The presence of Caroline, "a downright Miss," distracted Fanny's attention, and he teased the importunate visitor unmercifully; he and Brown "hated her and smoked her and baited her, and I think drove her away."

Of Fanny herself Keats had long observed every feature, word and movement. He would not reveal his inner mind to George, but he sent him a critical analysis: "Shall I give you Miss Brawn[e]? She is about my height,"—it was a fact of significance—"with a fine style of countenance of the length-en'd sort—she wants sentiment in every feature—she manages to make her hair look well—her nostrills are fine—though a little painful—he[r] mouth is bad and good—he[r] Profil is better than her full-face which indeed is not full but pale and thin without showing any bone—Her shape is very graceful and so are her movements—her Arms are good her hands badish—her feet tolerable—she is not seventeen—but she is ignorant—monstrous in her behaviour flying out in all directions, calling people such names—that I was forced lately to make use of the term *Minx*—this is I think no[t] from any innate vice but from a penchant she has for acting stylishly. I am however tired of such style and shall decline any more of it."

The criticism was only a clumsy decoy. It was written a week before Christmas and by that time Fanny had shown her affec tion unmistakably. For her, from the first moment, Keats had felt that entire love which alone could satisfy him. It was the almost religious love of Romeo and Juliet, and for Juliet he had long expressed his yearning; often he came to identify the Shakespearean love with his own. He had transfigured Fanny in his imagination, his passion creating in her the beauty which for him became the truth; and so she had come to be the Indian maid and the goddess, the fulfilment of *Endymion*, the very symbol of beauty, the reconciliation between real life and his poetic quest: "Why may I not speak of your Beauty, since without that I could never have lov'd you. I cannot conceive any beginning of such love as I have for you but Beauty. There may be a sort of love for which, without the least sneer at it, I have the highest respect and can admire it in others: but it has not the richness, the bloom, the full form, the enchantment of love after my own heart."[8]

Since mid December Keats had been living with Brown at Wentworth Place. He intended to follow Brown to Chichester for Christmas, but his recurrent sore throat led him to abandon the journey, and Mrs. Brawne invited him to spend Christmas Day at Elm Cottage. On Friday, December 25th, 1818, Keats proposed to Fanny Brawne.[9] It was, she wrote, "the happiest day I had ever then spent." She accepted him wholeheartedly.

## III

❖❖❖

SHE HAD NOT made a socially successful match: Keats offered her no worldly advantages. He had abandoned the safe profes sion of medicine for poetry, and *Endymion*, violently criticized in powerful magazines, lingered in the shops; there was consumption in his family, and he himself was frequently unwell; he could not yet make use of his brother's estate and he was unable to live on his own income.

To Mrs. Brawne, ambitious for her daughter, love weighed little against such disadvantages. Indeed (for Fanny was only eighteen) it might not be love at all: perhaps it was but the infatuation of a child, in time to be outgrown. Mrs. Brawne decided to give it time, to wait at least until Keats showed signs of enjoying a steadier future. She would not yet sanction the marriage, make Fanny an allowance, or ask Keats to live with them; and unless his prospects improved and she gave her legal consent a wedding would be impossible for the better part of three years.

Keats dined at Elm Cottage on the first day of 1819: to his brother he wrote that the party had been uneventful, and he made no mention of the betrothal; but in his high-spirited letter, with casual prodigality, he copied out *Fancy* and *Bards of Passion*; and "there is just room I see in this page to copy out a little thing I wrote off to some Music as it was playing."

The first "sort of rondeau," written in 1818, suggests none the less the inward delight with which he began the new year. The details of every season, enjoyed and anticipated, tumble in eager profusion from his mind, until his fancy enchants him with a vision of Fanny herself:

> O the Ravishment—the Bliss!
> Fancy has her there she is—
> Never fulsome, ever new,
> There she steps! and tell me who
> Has a Mistress so divine?

Fanny's happiness was broken only when Keats left for Chichester[10] late in January; he and Brown went on to

Bedhampton and soon their joint letter, full of cross-talk and
word-play, reached the Dilkes in London and was shown to
her. Keats asked to be remembered "to Wentworth Place and
Elm Cottage—not forgetting Millamant." He himself had
not forgotten her; he knew an intensity of joy beyond that
of common men. He celebrated his love in "a little Poem
call'd 'St. Agnes Eve.'"

## IV
❖❖❖

ST. AGNES' EVE falls on January 20th, about the date on which
Keats left Hampstead for Chichester, and as for the first time he
bade farewell to Fanny the legend was exquisitely suited to his
mind; for it was said that on that night a maiden would dream
about her future husband and that her phantom lover would
come to greet her.

The legend of St. Agnes' Eve might have been forgotten had
it not become the poet's own; but the love of Porphyro for
Madeline seems to be the dream-fulfilment of his love for
Fanny Brawne. "Beautiful name, that Magdalen," Keats had
written, and in its more harmonious form it keeps a religious
significance; the whole romance, like that of Romeo and Juliet,
appears almost sacred.

It is not surprising that Keats, who felt that Shakespeare
guided him, who expressed himself so often in a Shakespearean
phrase, should have seen his ideal love in *Romeo and Juliet*. Long
ago he had written that he yearned for the lips of Juliet, that he
would rather follow her into pandemonium than Imogen into
paradise, that he heartily wished himself "a Romeo to be
worthy of her." His instant recognition of his ideal in Fanny
Brawne had resembled Romeo's recognition of "true beauty"
at the Capulets' ball; and *The Eve of St. Agnes* comes at times
very close to the tragedy.

Even as Porphyro enters Madeline's house which is gay with revellers, the guests become in his mind

> . . . hot-blooded lords,
> Whose very dogs would execrations howl
> Against his lineage . . .

As Romeo had gazed on Juliet, unseen, so Porphyro, hidden in darkness, looks on Madeline and breaks and enters her dream. Romeo had seen Juliet glorious

> As is a winged messenger of heaven,

and Porphyro wakes Madeline with the words:

> And now, my love, my seraph fair, awake!
> Thou art my heaven, and I thine eremite.

Romeo had greeted his "dear saint," his "holy shrine," with the humble adoration of a pilgrim; Madeline, as she kneels beneath the emblazoned window, seems herself a saint,

> . . . a splendid angel, newly drest,
> Save wings, for heaven . . .

and with religious devotion Porphyro greets her:

> Ah, silver shrine, here will I take my rest
> After so many hours of toil and quest,
> A famish'd pilgrim,—saved by miracle.

Again, more than once and sometimes unconsciously, in Keats's poetry and in his letters to Fanny, he suggests this identification of his love. Madeline, "trembling in her soft and chilly nest," is the goddess who has slept in Keats's mind; the poem becomes an anthem in his elevation and purity of heart. In this spirit he had always loved Fanny Brawne, and in this spirit, assured of her love, he consummates his marriage:

> Ethereal, flush'd, and like a throbbing star
> Seen mid the sapphire heaven's deep repose
> Into her dream he melted, as the rose
> Blendeth its odour with the violet,—
> Solution sweet . . .

## V

✦✦✦

FANNY WAS parted from Keats within a month of their betrothal. Apart from her family and a very few intimate friends, no one was yet to know of the engagement; Mrs. Brawne continued to ask *émigrés* to Elm Cottage and to accept invitations for her daughter from local society. January was a festive month, and sewing and serious reading could not always exclude the pleasures of Hampstead and Woolwich.[11] Mrs. Brawne was fond of Keats, and as she "mingled in musical and literary society," she naturally talked about his writing; speaking of him with Mr. Lewis on the way to London one morning, she welcomed the opinion: "O, he is quite the little Poet." But she and Fanny's friend, Mrs. Rodd, "often dis-cussed the advisability or otherwise of Fanny's attachment to John Keats, whom they looked upon as an unsuccessful medical student and 'a mad boy'—the last Mrs. Brawne's own words."[12] Mrs. Rodd, herself the wife of the local surgeon, reminded Mrs. Brawne that Keats had abandoned a secure and profitable profession; while Fanny's aunts, who had married stable middle-class merchants, could see no future in his poetry. Even Mrs. Dilke, who was fond of him and believed in his poetry, still thought him "a very odd young man."

Early in February, Keats was at Wentworth Place. He had suffered intermittently from his throat for nearly a year. He had been unwell at Bedhampton, and had gone out only two or three times while he was there; now he was forced to remain indoors. Fanny often came to see him, and sometimes she met his friends.

Jane and Mariane Reynolds were staying with the Dilkes. Nowadays Keats found the sisters very dull, and perhaps Jane noticed and resented his lack of interest, for she was twenty-seven and had always been fond of him. She took a spiteful dislike to

Fanny, spoke slightingly about her to Mrs. Dilke, and hoped to break what she called "a most unhappy connexion." She led her brother John to speak of Fanny's triviality, and the Rey, nolds' active unpleasantness did not pass unnoticed. Keats recognized them as "these Laughers, who envy you for your Beauty, who would have God, bless'd me from you for ever: who were plying me with disencouragements eternally." "Every day I live," Fanny came to write, "I find out more of their malice against me."

She met Severn,* too, on her visits to Wentworth Place. It has been suggested that he was "not at all deeply, or even favourably, impressed,"[13] and that he considered her "a cold and conventional mistress"; but later, in a picture in Rome, he found an extraordinary likeness to her: "There is a beautiful portrait of Miss Brawne by Titian in the 'sacred and profane Love' . . . this figure always delighted me & I used to visit the Borghese Palace often to look at it as her portrait." As he was not allowed to suspect that Fanny and Keats were betrothed, she tried to be indifferent in his presence; but he came in time to think her "a most lovely and accomplished girl," and to Monckton Milnes, nearly thirty years later, he wrote: "Miss Brawn was devotedly attached to Keats & his fame."

Severn was a handsome man of twenty-five. Brown, in his thirties, was rather bald and already inclined to corpulence; but his travels in Russia, his literary tastes, his wit and irre, pressible joviality made him highly entertaining. His grand, daughter writes: "My grandfather did not like Fanny Brawne; he thought her superficial and vain, and he considered that her flirtatious manner, in the company of every man she met, accounted for Keats's jealousy." It seems, however, that Brown himself paid Fanny some attention, and though she would not encourage him, once at least he sent her a valentine.[14]

It was natural that Fanny should be admired; and as Keats could not dance and was too unwell to take her out himself, she

went to parties with army officers. Through the Dilkes and her
mother's wide circle of friends she received many invitations.
She could not be expected to remain always at home, refusing
to go to the opera and rejecting quadrilles; and at times, in that
early spring of 1819, when Keats reflected on her constant
gaiety and his own hindering, persistent illness, his anxiety
could no longer be restrained:

Ah! dearest love, sweet home of all my fears,
And hopes, and joys, and panting miseries,—
To night, if I may guess, thy beauty wears
A smile of such delight,
As brilliant and as bright,
As when with ravished, aching, vassal eyes,
Lost in soft amaze,
I gaze, I gaze!

Who now, with greedy looks, eats up my feast?
What stare outfaces now my silver moon!
Ah! keep that hand unravished at the least;
Let, let the amorous burn—
But, pr'ythee, do not turn
The current of your heart from me so soon.
O! save, in charity,
The quickest pulse for me.

Save it for me, sweet love! though music breathe
Voluptuous visions into the warm air;
Though swimming through the dance's dangerous wreath;
Be like an April day,
Smiling and cold and gay,
A temperate lily, temperate as fair;
Then, Heaven! there will be
A warmer June for me.

\*        \*        \*

Ah! if you prize my subdued soul above
The poor, the fading, brief pride of an hour;
Let none profane my Holy See of love,
Or with a rude hand break

> The sacramental cake:
> Let none else touch the just new-budded flower;
> If not—may my eyes close,
> Love! on their last repose.

The *Ode to Fanny*, with its reminiscence of Romeo's first greeting to Juliet, may belong to the early months of the betrothal; and on February 13th, just before St. Valentine's Day, Keats began "a little thing call'd the 'eve of St. Mark.'"

## VI

❖❖❖

IT IS SAID that on April 25th, the Eve of St. Mark, those who keep vigil at a church door will see the ghosts of all who are to die within the year, and that those who rake the ashes in a fire will find upon them next morning the footprints of the doomed. Perhaps Keats intended that in his poem both omens should appear, for Bertha lives "in the old Minster-square," and it is by the fireside that she reads the legend of St. Mark, and learns of the procession of those who are to die.

Here the fragment ends; and that it remains a fragment was, to W. M. Rossetti, "the greatest grievance of which the admirers of Keats have to complain." Its hundred lines show the spontaneity and simplicity of his best work. Seven months after he began it Keats still wondered if he would finish it, but Dante Rossetti, forecasting the rest of the story, surmised that Bertha would go to the Minster porch and see her sick and absent lover enter but not return; perhaps, too, she would find, on the ashes of her fire, the imprint of his feet. That, in all probability, was the ending which Keats had intended; it was a portent to Fanny that his love might not be fulfilled, a doubt of the complete and surpassing happiness of *The Eve of St. Agnes*, and the portent became in time too real and too sad for expression.

Even now it seemed that his betrothal might be prolonged

indefinitely; and when Fanny repeated that it would not be unpleasant to wait for a few years, she was only making the best of necessity. Indeed, if she knew of his reckless generosity to others, her hopes of marriage in the near future could hardly have been encouraged: Keats was involved with Abbey and his lawyers and trying to draw some of his money for Haydon, and he had resolved not to write for the sake of writing, but from knowledge or experience which might perhaps be gained from "many years of reflection . . . with respect to my livelihood, I will not write for it,—for I will not run with that most vulgar of all crowds, the literary." He considered, possibly at the Brawnes' suggestion, whether he should study medicine at Edinburgh, but it seemed uncongenial; he felt indolent, he rose late in the morning, and once, despite himself, he fell asleep after dinner. "I cannot bare a day annihilated in that manner . . . I do not know what I did on Monday—nothing—nothing—nothing—I wish this was anything extraordinary." Yet his lassitude seemed to be beyond control: poetry, ambition, love itself appeared as lifeless as figures on a Greek vase, and death, he wrote, had become the crowning joy. In this faith he wrote the sonnet *Why did I laugh to-night?* His moods in March were not easy for a girl of eighteen to understand.

Early in April, however, the "old dog trot" of Hampstead life was broken: the Dilkes had decided to send Charley to Westminster, and they moved to London to be near the school. Soon afterwards the Brawnes' furniture arrived at Wentworth Place.

## VII

❖❖❖

IT SEEMS strange that Mrs. Brawne should have chosen to be Keats's next door neighbour; but perhaps she felt that proxi/mity would decide the strength or weakness of her daughter's attachment, make Keats more determined to improve his prospects, to abandon his "mad craze" for poetry and choose a reliable career. Henceforward Fanny saw Keats almost every day: the Brawnes' dog, Carlo, or one of their cats, might wander into his sitting-room and need to be returned; she enjoyed the luxuriant common garden, and often she came to his open window to greet him or to bring an invitation from her mother. Brown watched the Brawnes' behaviour in his usual jocular fashion, and within a few days of their arrival Keats noted that "Brown this morning is writing some Spenserian stansas against Mrs. Miss Brawne and me." He answered by writing a Spenserian satire on Brown.

On Sundays and school holidays another observer, John Finch,* would arrive from his school at Norway House, off the High Street. He was Fanny's cousin, eleven years old, and he criticized her conduct with the acerbity and freedom of a close relation. She would (or so he professed to remember in his eighties) talk French to foreign visitors: "Keats could not talk French as they could and their conversation with his fiancée in a language he could not understand was a source of continual disagreement between them. Keats thought she talked and flirted and danced too much with them, but his remonstrances were all unheeded by Miss Brawne." Keats, however, understood some French and it seems unlikely that he made his feelings public; it is more probable that John Finch heightened his memories to suit the popular Victorian tradition.

As April advanced, Fanny and Keats, avoiding company, often walked across the Heath: they would go to the summit by the Spaniards' Road to see the sand diggers at work and the laden carts lumbering off to London; they would walk on past the cottage at the end of Judges' Walk to which Mrs. Siddons had come to cure her rheumatism, and past Joanna and Agnes Baillie's house: in the clement weather the sisters had ventured down their little flagged walk, and, dressed alike in grey silk, stood talking in the garden, probably of past visitors like

Miss Edgeworth and Mr. Scott. But Fanny herself concentrated all Keats's attention: in her presence his thoughts never wandered from her. He could not think of her "without some sort of energy," and her frequent company, the sound of her voice next door, and, at first, the continual awareness of her presence, distracted his mind from poetry. He began to dread a barren poetic future, and considered trying some other career; in mid-April he decided to live in Westminster.

Whether he could finally leave Hampstead he must have doubted; no more is heard of his decision. But his poetry was not long to be delayed. He had met Coleridge, and their conversation and the fifth canto of the *Inferno*, which Keats had repeatedly read, had slumbered in his mind; he dreamed that he was in the same region of Hell. He tried to express his emotion in the Hermes Sonnet, and it seems to have been the first sign of returning inspiration, for on April 21st, in the course of a letter, he wrote "with headlong impetuosity" *La Belle Dame Sans Merci*. It was the "ancient ditty, long since mute," which Porphyro had played to Madeline, and perhaps it reflected now a passing melancholy mood, a vague thought of his own irresistible vassalage. *La Belle Dame Sans Merci* was immediately followed by a *Chorus of Faeries*, and by the end of the month his journal letter to America contained another six poems, including the sonnet *To Sleep* and the first of the great Odes, the *Ode to Psyche*.

One morning in May, under the mulberry tree, he set down his *Ode to a Nightingale*, and that same month he wrote the *Ode on a Grecian Urn*. The Odes make no direct allusion to Fanny, but they suggest the ecstasy of passion, the transience of earthly beauty, the perfection of unchanging love "for ever warm and still to be enjoyed." They reflect more than a mood, for they were written within a few weeks of Fanny's coming to Wentworth Place; they show that after the first unsettled days, and while he was living near her, seeing her frequently and certain of her love, Keats entered the six most fertile weeks in his poetic life and touched what, to many, is the height of his poetry.

But the idyllic period was not to last. He would soon need to leave Hampstead, as Brown would let his house for the summer. Trying to forget the past, he burnt his old letters and memoranda, and thought of becoming a surgeon on an East Indiaman. Perhaps the suggestion came from George Darling, the friend of Keats's publisher and the medical adviser of Haydon, for Dr. Darling had himself held such an appoint/ ment; or perhaps Mrs. Brawne, who still considered Keats as an unsuccessful medical student, told him that he should marry when he had established himself in his old profession. But he preferred to conquer indolence and "strive at some grand Poem—than be in a dunderheaded Indiaman. . . . I must choose between despair and Energy—I choose the latter."

Throughout June he remained unsettled in his mind. His sore throat returned, his financial affairs grew so precarious[15] that he thought of working with an apothecary; but Brown per/ suaded him to try poetry once more and lent him money for his immediate needs, and he determined to shake off his indolent "1819 temper." "My purpose is now to make one more attempt in the Press—if that fail, 'ye hear no more of me.'"

His love for Fanny had never been stronger: six months after their betrothal, his passion remained unbounded, his happiness was still centred in her, his vassalage was more certain; and despite his recklessness and other faults which time had re/ vealed to her, Fanny loved him deeply. But a few days before he left Hampstead he told her that he would not return unless his fate "turned up Pam or at least a Court/card"; it would be selfish to bind her to an uncertain future, the "unpromising morning" of his life.

On June 27th, he was on the Portsmouth coach, on his way to the Isle of Wight. For the first time he had left Fanny indefinitely, and within two days he wrote a letter to her; but he had no chance to post it, and afterwards he was glad: "'twas too much like one out of Ro[u]sseau's Heloise."

## VIII

*❖❖❖*

IN THE FIRST week of July Fanny heard from him. He was staying in Shanklin; the cottage was pleasant, the country beautiful, but all his enjoyment was lost in the remembrance of her, and sometimes his longing grew uncontrollable:

> Ask yourself my love whether you are not very cruel to have so en-
> trammelled me, so destroyed my freedom. Will you confess this in
> the Letter you must write immediately and do all you can to console
> me in it—make it rich as a draught of poppies to intoxicate me—
> write the softest words and kiss them that I may at least touch my
> lips where yours have been. For myself I know not how to express
> my devotion to so fair a form: I want a brighter word than bright, a
> fairer word than fair. I almost wish we were butterflies and liv'd but
> three summer days—three such days with you I could fill with more
> delight than fifty common years could ever contain.

Yet even now he professed to doubt the wholeheartedness of her love:

> Though I could centre my Happiness in you, I cannot expect to
> engross your heart so entirely—indeed if I thought you felt as much
> for me as I do for you at this moment I do not think I could restrain
> myself from seeing you again tomorrow for the delight of one embrace.
> But no—I must live upon hope and Chance. In case of the worst
> that can happen, I shall still love you—but what hatred shall I have
> for another!

Though he himself had told her that she might not see him again he was haunted by fears that she might receive attention from other men; in his jealousy he was always afraid of her being "a little inclined to the Cressid," and as a poet he feared to find a difference between reality and the goddess in his mind. From the first moment he had idealized his love, demanding not merely the affection of a woman but a passion, poetic, omnipotent, the equal of his own, the sacred passion of Juliet, the divine love of Diana.

Fanny was human enough to feel that his love need not exclude all other admiration; she was eighteen and enjoyed the pleasures of her age. She was, however, blessed with remark‑ able understanding, and despite his moods of hurtful suspicion which later bordered on insult, she loved him constantly. She answered his letter almost by return. She was afraid that he loved her too much for her physical attraction and too little for her deeper, permanent self, and she asked him to speak less of her beauty; and having corrected him, she feared that he would doubt the entirety of her love. Keats had repeated that he might not return to London, and she wondered if it were Abbey, or perhaps the Reynolds family, who would decide whether he saw her again. She told him of the comet she had watched from Wentworth Place and, thinking of omens, added that she had had a dream; but what she had dreamed she deliberately with‑ held, for she wanted him to write soon. Keats, who wrote to her every Thursday, answered her:

All my thoughts, my unhappiest days and nights have I find not at all cured me of my love of Beauty, but made it so intense that I am miserable that you are not with me. . . . You mention "horrid people" and ask me whether it depend upon them, whether I see you again. Do understand me, my love, in this. I have so much of you in my heart that I must turn Mentor when I see a chance of harm beffaling you. I would never see any thing but Pleasure in your eyes, love on your lips, and Happiness in your steps. . . . You say you are affraid I shall think you do not love me—in saying this you make me ache the more to be near you . . . and here I must confess, that, (since I am on that subject,) I love you the more in that I believe you have liked me for my own sake and for nothing else. I have met with women

4

whom I really think would like to be married to a Poem and to be
given away by a Novel. I have seen your Comet. . . . What was
your dream? Tell it me and I will tell you the interpretation thereof.

But despite his fervour Fanny remained afraid that he might not
return, and this constant thought and the strain of the last few
months had made her ill. She wrote to him promptly, and
Keats received her news with the unconcealed selfish pleasure
of a lover:

> If through me illness have touched you (but it must be with a very
> gentle hand) I must be selfish enough to feel a little glad at it. Will
> you forgive me this? . . . I will see you in a month at most, though no
> one but yourself should see me; if it be but for an hour.

William Dilke, half a century later, gave the Victorian
opinion that Fanny "made the advances to Keats without really
caring much for him." But she, who would allow none of her
friends a key to her emotions, remained, even after Keats's
promise, ill with strain. When Brown left Wentworth Place
towards the end of the month, she was still unwell. She was
afraid that she might have seemed to show undue favour to
Severn, and hastened to assure Keats that she had made no
comparison, and she asked him to write on Saturday, the
twenty-fourth. His letter would have reached Wentworth
Place by Samuel's birthday, and allowed her to enjoy her
brother's festivities. Keats does not seem to have understood the
request, but he wrote to her on the night of the twenty-fifth:

> Brown to my sorrow confirms the account you give of your ill health.
> You cannot conceive how I ache to be with you: how I would die
> for one hour—for what is in the world? . . . Perhaps I am too vehe-
> ment, then fancy me on my knees, especially when I mention a part
> of your Letter which hurt me; you say speaking of Mr. Severn "but
> you must be satisfied in knowing that I admired you much more than
> your friend". My dear love. . . . I am not a thing to be admired. . . .
> You are, I love you; all I can bring you is a swooning admiration of
> your Beauty. . . . I have two luxuries to brood over in my walks,
> your Loveliness and the hour of my death. O that I could have

possession of them both in the same minute. I hate the world: it batters too much the wings of my self-will, and would I could take a sweet poison from your lips to send me out of it. From no others would I take it. . . . I will imagine you Venus tonight and pray, pray, pray to your star like a He[a]then.

*Romeo and Juliet* had again entered his mind. Asking to die by taking poison from Fanny's lips, he echoed the cry of Juliet as she woke from her trance, and asking to possess his love and death together, he suggested the words of Romeo in the Capulet vault:

> Arms, take your last embrace! and lips, O you
> The doors of breath, seal with a righteous kiss
> A dateless bargain to engrossing death!

That he too might die in a last eternal embrace, "half-passion-less and so swoon on to death," was his prayer to Venus in the first version of the Bright Star Sonnet. It was one of the poems which Fanny herself loved best, and she copied it in the Dante which he had given her.

She was already anxious because the letter came late; and Keats's longing for death filled her with fear. She answered at once that she wanted no more letters like it. In mid-July he had promised to see her within a month, and she wanted him in Hampstead for her birthday. She asked him after his health, and told him that she had visited the fair; but whether or not she felt better she did not say. At the end of July she was bitterly unhappy.

It was August; the haymakers came from the Fens to help on the farms in Hampstead. Horses stretched their yearning necks to drink out of the troughs; and householders who, unlike the Brawnes, had no cistern in the house, were forced to send frequently for washing water from the ponds at Red Lion Hill or South End Green. The only safe drinking water came from the well in the Conduit Fields, and as Fanny sat under a laden plum tree in the garden of Wentworth Place, she would see Jack Rough, the water-carrier, striding past the hedge, swinging his heavy buckets to whatever tune he was humming. At six in the evening she would hear the watchman fire his gun and blow his horn at Ken Wood, and about closing time the barman at the Spaniards Tavern would fire a horse-pistol to warn customers and malcontents; the local watchman, who guarded Wentworth Place and Downshire Hill, continued his cry into the night, and the one at Ken Wood repeated his signals at six o'clock every morning. The hot and restless nights gave Fanny time for thought; and wherever she went in day-time, in the shade of the elms along Millfield Lane, down the Spaniards' Road or towards the old farm at West End, Hampstead reminded her of Keats. Soon after her birthday she heard from him.

He would obey her and write no more of his longing for love and death: indeed he was too busy to write love-letters at all. He was forcing her from his thoughts, though at night, when he left his tragedy, she returned only the stronger to his fevered mind:

> So you intend to hold me to my promise of seeing you in a short time. I shall keep it with as much sorrow as gladness: for I am not one of the Paladins of old who livd upon water grass and smiles for years together. . . . I will flit to you and back. I will stay very little while, for as I am in a train of writing now I fear to disturb it.

He had been gone for nearly eight weeks and she had written regularly and thought of him often; by his severe change of tone she was understandably hurt. She answered that she would not make him come to Wentworth Place: he could please himself whether or not he saw her.

About a week later she received his answer from Winchester. "Believe in the first Letters I wrote you: I assure you I felt as I wrote—I could not do so now." Poetry, uneasiness, his "unguess'd fate" veiled her from him, he had no time for brooding;

indeed he could not have borne the jealousies which used to haunt him. He would not now come to Hampstead:

> I would feign, as my sails are set, sail on without an interruption for a Brace of Months longer. . . . This Page as my eye skims over it I see is excessively unloverlike and ungallant—I cannot help it—I am no officer in yawning quarters; no Parson-romeo. . . . You say I may do as I please—I do not think with any conscience I can; my cash resourses are for the present stopp'd; I fear for some time. . . . You see how I go on—like so many strokes of a Hammer. I cannot help it—I am impell'd, driven to it. I am not happy enough for silken Phrases, and silver sentences. I can no more use soothing words to you than if I were at this moment engaged in a charge of Cavalry.

Poetry mastered him, he could not afford to be "uncrystal- lized and dissolved" by thinking of her, and deliberately he was forcing her from his mind. She understood that only his despondency made him hurt her, that "he never could have addressed an unkind expression, much less a violent one, to any human being"; but in this flint-worded letter there was much to understand and forgive.

Within a week of meeting her, Keats had recognized that he had lost all hope of independence, that he must offer

> Vows of my slavery, my giving up,
> My sudden adoration, my great love!

Now and bitterly he told his publisher: "I equally dislike the favour of the public with the love of a woman—they are both a cloying treacle to the wings of independence." Driven by nature and ambition, the persistent fear of a brief life, to write the poetry within him, he must be free.

He was threatened with a Chancery suit and could make no demands of Abbey; his considerable loans had not been repaid, and Brown had long advanced him money. Now, late in August, he asked Taylor for enough to last him through the summer. He had grown anxious about his physical condition:

"I feel my body too weak to support me to the height"; yet already, through exertion, he lived in a rarefied atmosphere, a spiritual world in which men and women were shadows, the only world in which he could write the highest poetry; "and that is all I care for, all I live for."

Early in September, repayments and a sum from his pub-lisher improved his finances for a time. Since he had come to Winchester he had finished *Lamia*; he was now revising *The Eve of St. Agnes* and studying Greek and Italian. Brown had already gone "to Chichester and Bedhampton avisiting," and he was to be by himself in Winchester for three weeks. Assured of an ample sum of money, left alone with his books in a tranquil cathedral city, he might in that brief period have accomplished much; but on September 10th, as he was "closely employed in reading and composition," he heard that George had speculated and come near to ruin. Keats took a place in the London coach that night, hoping, with Abbey's help, to secure money for George. He wanted to publish *The Eve of St. Agnes* immediately, but his publisher considered it unwise.

Keats had written the poem in January, and since the early days of his betrothal his future had become increasingly un-certain. He knew that illness and growing financial insecurity might bar him finally from marriage; he had been betrothed for more than nine months, and he could not live indefinitely on imagination. He revised *The Eve of St. Agnes*: it now became the expression of violent desire.

Keats told Woodhouse, who recorded his strong disap-proval, that he did not want women to read his poetry, that he wrote for men, "& that if in the former poem there was an opening for a doubt what took place, it was his fault for not writing clearly and comprehensively—that he shd despise a man who would be such an eunuch in sentiment as to leave a maid, with that Character about her, in such a situation:

& shod despise himself to write about it &c &c &c—and all this sort of Keats-like rhodomontade." Taylor, to whom Wood- house was writing, was deeply shocked; and if, he replied, his fears were confirmed on reading the new version, he would have to admire the poem under some other imprint.

Since he left Hampstead, more than two months ago, Keats had tried constantly to suppress his passion; Woodhouse and Taylor, unwittingly, had learned of his struggle. Perhaps Fanny herself, from his letters and his long silence, had under- stood his purpose.

> I love you too much to venture to Hampstead [he explained to her before he returned to Winchester], I feel it is not paying a visit, but venturing into a fire. Que feraije? as the french novel writers say in fun, and I in earnest: really what can I do? Knowing well that my life must be passed in fatigue and trouble, I have been endeavouring to wean myself from you: for to myself alone what can be much of a misery? As far as they regard myself I can despise all events: but I cannot cease to love you. . . . I shall return to Winchester tomorrow; whence you shall hear from me in a few days. I am a Coward, I cannot bear the pain of being happy: 'tis out of the question: I must admit no thought of it.

The letter was an effect of his brother's misfortune: to George he wrote: "I feel I can bear anything—any misery, even im- prisonment—so long as I have neither wife nor child." He was preparing to tell Fanny that he would finally leave Wentworth Place. He was still haunted by the apprehension of early death; he would not burst the grape against his palate, nor taste the transience of happiness.

For some days the decision hovered in his mind, but at last, by September 21st, when he casually sent Woodhouse the *Ode to Autumn*, he had determined to live in Westminster and write for periodicals. He asked Dilke to find him rooms. On September 23rd, firmly, he wrote to Brown: "At the end of another year you shall applaud me, not for verses but for con- duct. If you live at Hampstead next winter—I like******** and I cannot help it. On that account I had better not live there."

Early in October Dilke found him rooms at 25, College Street, Westminster, and by Friday, October 8th, Keats was in London. Perhaps the Dilkes or Brown had told the Brawnes of his coming, and an invitation from Fanny awaited him; perhaps he intended to fetch his possessions and leave her indefinitely. However that may be, on Sunday, October 10th, after an absence of exactly fifteen weeks, he returned to Hampstead. The hedges were sparkling with their abundant berries, the fruit on the trees was filled with ripeness to the core, and the garden at Wentworth Place shone with late flowers.

Fanny had never been so loving or so kind.

> My sweet Girl,
>     I am living today in yesterday: I was in a complete fa[s]cination all day. I feel myself at your mercy. Write me ever so few lines and tell me you will never for ever be less kind to me than yesterday—. You dazzled me. There is nothing in the world so bright and deli-cate. When Brown came out with that seemingly true story again[s]t me last night, I felt it would be death to me if you had ever believed it—though against any one else I could muster up my obstinacy. Before I knew Brown could disprove it I was for the moment miserable. When shall we pass a day alone? I have had a thousand kisses, for which with my whole soul I thank love—but if you should deny me the thousand and first—'twould put me to the proof how great a misery I could live through. If you should ever carry your threat yesterday into execution—believe me 'tis not my pride, my vanity or any petty passion would torment me—really 'twould hurt my heart—I could not bear it. I have seen Mrs. Dilke this morning; she says she will come with me any fine day.
>                                         Ever yours
>                                         John Keats
> Ah hertè mine!

The period of Keats's finest work and most intensive study was ended when he visited Hampstead on October 10th. It

would be untrue to say that he could not write when Fanny
was near him; he had written *La Belle Dame Sans Merci* and
three at least of the Odes after the Brawnes had moved to Wentworth Place: Fanny may well have been in the garden while he
wrote the *Ode to a Nightingale*. But now that he had lived "like
a Hermit" for so long, and had returned to her at last to learn of
her deep and constant love, his powers of concentration were
dispelled. His yearning for her could not be restrained:

> The day is gone, and all its sweets are gone!
>    Sweet voice, sweet lips, soft hand, and softer breast,
> Warm breath, light whisper, tender semi-tone,
>    Bright eyes, accomplish'd shape, and lang'rous waist!
> Faded the flower and all its budded charms,
>    Faded the sight of beauty from my eyes,
> Faded the shape of beauty from my arms,
>    Faded the voice, warmth, whiteness, paradise—
> Vanish'd unseasonably at shut of eve,
>    When the dusk holiday—or holinight
> Of fragrant-curtain'd love begins to weave
>    The woof of darkness thick, for hid delight;
> But, as I've read love's missal through to-day,
> He'll let me sleep, seeing I fast and pray.

The love of Keats, like that of Romeo and Porphyro, became
once more religious in its fervour, and Fanny answered his
letter, boundlessly happy. Her note arrived at College Street on
Wednesday as he was writing to her again:

My dearest Girl,
   This moment I have set myself to copy some verses out fair. I
cannot proceed with any degree of content. I must write you a line
or two and see if that will assist in dismissing you from my Mind
for ever so short a time. Upon my Soul I can think of nothing else.
The time is passed when I had power to advise and warn you against
the unpromising morning of my Life. My love has made me selfish.
I cannot exist without you. I am forgetful of every thing but seeing
you again—my Life seems to stop there—I see no further. You

have absorb'd me. I have a sensation at the present moment as though I was dissolving—I should be exquisitely miserable without the hope of soon seeing you. I should be affraid to separate myself far from you. My sweet Fanny, will your heart never change? My love, will it? I have no limit now to my love—You[r] note came in just here—I cannot be happier away from you. 'Tis richer than an Argosy of Pearles. Do not threat me even in jest. I have been astonished that Men could die Martyrs for religion—I have shudder'd at it. I shudder no more—I could be martyr'd for my Religion—Love is my religion—I could die for that. I could die for you. My Creed is Love and you are its only tenet. You have ravish'd me away by a Power I cannot resist; and yet I could resist till I saw you; and ever since I have seen you I have endeavoured often "to reason against the reasons of my Love". I can do that no more—the pain would be too great. My love is selfish. I cannot breathe without you.

On Saturday, from Wentworth Place, he wrote to his sister, explaining that he had "returned to Hampstead being induced to it by the habit I have acquired of this room I am now in." He spent the week-end at Hampstead; and the dream in his Hermes Sonnet which he had longed to dream again, the magic love of *La Belle Dame Sans Merci*, were, in the "three days dream" of Keats, made real to him. "He remained in his new lodging two days (I think no more) and lived again with me," wrote Brown, years later, "not aware, as I was, of his incapability of living in solitude, and distant from the young lady in Hampstead who had won his heart."

The three days' dream at Wentworth Place ended on Monday. On Tuesday morning, from the Dilkes', Keats sent a note to Fanny:

Mrs. Dilke I should think will tell you that I purpose living at Hampstead. I must impose chains upon myself. I shall be able to do nothing. I sho[u]ld like to cast the die for Love or death. I have no Patience with any thing else.

## IX

❖❖❖

ON WEDNESDAY he was again at Wentworth Place. His
return, for which Fanny had longed throughout the summer,
could not now give her entire happiness; he was greatly
changed. His poetic fervour had gone, he tried a drama and
abandoned it, he hoped in vain to write another poem like *The
Eve of St. Agnes*; but his muse remained low-spirited, and in
the November mornings he could only write a comic fairy
poem, *The Cap and Bells*, while in the evenings he recast
*Hyperion*. His work, Brown recalled, was constantly inter-
rupted "by a circumstance which it is needless to mention."

> What can I do to drive away
> Remembrance from my eyes? for they have seen,
> Aye, an hour ago, my brilliant Queen!
> Touch has a memory. O say, love, say,
> What can I do to kill it and be free
> In my old liberty?
> When every fair one that I saw was fair,
> Enough to catch me in but half a snare,
> Not keep me there:
> When, howe'er poor or particolour'd things,
> My muse had wings,
> And ever ready was to take her course
> Whither I bent her force,
> Unintellectual, yet divine to me;—
> Divine, I say!—what sea-bird o'er the sea
> Is a philosopher the while he goes
> Winging along where the great water throes? . . .
>
> O, for some sunny spell
> To dissipate the shadows of this hell!
> Say they are gone,—with the new dawning light
> Steps forth my lady bright!
> O, let me once more rest
> My soul upon that dazzling breast!

Let once again these aching arms be plac'd,
The tender gaolers of thy waist!
And let me feel that warm breath here and there
To spread a rapture in my very hair,—
O, the sweetness of the pain!
Give me those lips again!
Enough! Enough! it is enough for me
To dream of thee!

Made apprehensive by his brother's misfortune, his own
uncertain health, his barren mind, he could no longer con-
centrate on serious poetry, and his mental suffering became
dreadful to witness. He had lent some of his money to friends,
without prospect of repayment, and had now not enough on
which to live; his hopes of fame and happiness sank to nothing.
The nearness of Fanny herself, the very strength and constancy
of her affection could but increase his pain. At times he was
too silent and at times too restive, and he began to be reckless of
his health. Secretly he took laudanum to keep up his spirits;
only by chance was this discovered, and he promised Brown
not to take more.

On Christmas Day Fanny would have been betrothed to
Keats for a year. She had spent the long summer in loneliness
and uncertainty, and now that she was with him every day she
could not heal his suffering. Though she concealed her feelings
she felt the strain of the love which was increasingly disapproved by her family and unknown, still, to some of her
friends. To Keats, whose passion was beyond that of men,
the indefinite betrothal had become intolerable. Talking of
Severn's painting, he wrote: "You had best put me into your
Cave of despair," and to Rice he sent a story of a pregnant
woman which reflected his own increasing misery. As
December grew colder he felt unwell again and had to remain
indoors, while the season brought Fanny invitations which he
could not share and attentions which he was powerless to

prevent. Poetry and ambition had abandoned him, love was omnipotent, and time was pressing upon him; the common range of emotions could not comprehend his anguish:

> I cry your mercy—pity—love!—aye, love!
>   Merciful love that tantalises not,
> One-thoughted, never-wandering, guileless love,
>   Unmask'd, and being seen—without a blot!
> O! let me have thee whole,—all—all—be mine!
>   That shape, that fairness, that sweet minor zest
> Of love, your kiss,—those hands, those eyes divine,
>   That warm, white, lucent, million-pleasured breast,—
> Yourself—your soul—in pity give me all,
>   Withhold no atom's atom or I die,
> Or living on perhaps, your wretched thrall,
>   Forget, in the mist of idle misery,
> Life's purposes,—the palate of my mind
> Losing its gust, and my ambition blind!

To his sister he wrote that his hopes of literary success were better than ever; but he was only preparing his old poems for publication and heightening *Otho the Great*. He was too fearful of the weather to venture to Walthamstow, for cold or exertion still affected his throat and he had seen fit to take the advice of his doctor.

Early in the New Year the Dilkes gave "a pianoforte hop," at which George, who had just arrived on business from America, introduced his brother to an American called Hart. Keats liked him moderately and they

> began talking about english and american ladies—The Miss Reynolds and some of their friends made not a very enticing row opposite us. I bade him mark them and form his Judgement of them—I told him I hated Englishmen because they were the only Men I knew.

Keats tried manfully to sit near Jane and Mariane and talk to them, but to no purpose; they were now worse than dull, he could forecast their conversation, and he was afraid to speak to them "for fear of some sickly reiteration of Phrase or Sentiment."

Such formal politeness and evident disapproval did not increase Jane's sympathy for Fanny. Moreover, from Keats's
sudden hatred of Englishmen and of a certain Scot who was
also at the party, one feels that Fanny was socially successful.
George praised her appearance and Dilke admired her vivacity;
she danced well, talked with animation and listened with
unusual intelligence, and the Scottish teacher, a Mr. Webster,
who also lived in Hampstead, too evidently appreciated her
conversation: "Some people you must have observed," wrote
Keats, "have a most unpleasant effect upon you when you see
them speaking in profile—this Scotchman is the most accom-
plish'd fellow in this way I ever met with. The effect was
complete—it went down like a dose of bitters."

While George remained in England, there was considerable
entertainment at Wentworth Place, and once Fanny appeared
in "a tasty headdress of the age of Charles the 2nd.," to the
admiration of George and Severn. Keats would have liked to
see his young sister in Hampstead, and several times during
January Fanny asked her to stay: "I used," she told her later,
"to anticipate the pleasure I should feel in showing every kindness and attention in my power to you." But the indulgence of a
visit from Fanny Keats was not granted, and on January 28th
George boarded the Liverpool coach on his way to America.
He left Keats only £40 in notes, and, according to Brown,[16]
about £20 in debt.

## X

THE SUN HAD been shining on the snow, making, wrote
Keats, "a prettier candy than we have on twelvth-cakes." In the
first days of February came a thaw, and on February 3rd he
went to London.

That night at eleven o'clock, Brown remembered, he came

home, "in a state that looked like fierce intoxication. Such a state in him, I knew, was impossible; it therefore was the more fearful. I asked hurriedly, 'What is the matter?—you are fevered?' 'Yes, yes,' he answered, 'I was on the outside of the stage this bitter day till I was severely chilled.' . . . He mildly and instantly yielded to my request that he should go to bed. . . . On entering the cold sheets, he slightly coughed, and I heard him say, 'That is blood from my mouth. . . . Bring me the candle, Brown; and let me see this blood.' After regarding it steadfastly, he looked up in my face, with a calmness of counʹtenance that I can never forget, and said—'I know the colour of that blood;—it is arterial blood . . . that drop of blood is my deathʹwarrant;—I must die.'"

Fanny wrote later that she had seen Keats every day for more than twelve months before he left England; her statement cannot be taken literally, but she sat with him often now, and witʹnessed his physical and mental suffering. To his young sister Keats belittled his illness, but this pain of mind continued beyond belief; and in midʹFebruary, gently, he warned Fanny herself that he might not be able to marry her. She was already unwell and now she was silent with unhappiness. When she had left him she wondered if her silence had seemed cold, and wrote at once to assure him of her love. This note she brought round herself, and he sent her one in answer:

> I wish I had read your note [he replied] before you went last night that I might have assured you how far I was from suspecting any coldness. You had a just right to be a little silent to one who speaks so plainly to you. You must believe—you shall, you will—that I can do nothing, say nothing, think nothing of you but what has its spring in the Love which has so long been my pleasure and torment. On the night I was taken ill—when so violent a rush of blood came to my Lungs that I felt nearly suffocated—I assure you I felt it possible I might not survive, and at that moment though[t] of nothing but you.

But though she had not been told of his blunt conviction, the thought of losing Keats disturbed Fanny unceasingly. His offers to free her from her betrothal always filled her with grief; each evening she sent him a written good-night to put under his pillow, and the affection which she hid from friends she gave to him, heartfelt:

> How hurt I should have been [he wrote, when she had refused to leave him] had you ever acceded to what is, notwithstanding, very reasonable! How much the more do I love you from the general result! . . . My greatest torment since I have known you has been the fear of you being a little inclined to the Cressid; but that suspicion I dismiss utterly and remain happy in the surety of your Love, which I assure you is as much a wonder to me as a delight.

In mid-February he was able to walk in the garden; but he remained on a lowering diet and his improvement did not last. Again he grew feverish and the doctors warned him against all exertion. Throughout his illness Fanny had stayed at home to be near him and to encourage him by her presence; but now, despondent and unable to see her often, he told her not to remain indefinitely in Hampstead, and hinted more boldly at the larger freedom which might be forced upon her:

> Let me not longer detain you from going to Town—there may be no end to this imprisoning of you. . . . You know our situation—what hope is there if I should be recoverd ever so soon—my very health will not suffer me to make any great exertion. I am reccommended not even to read poetry, much less write it. I wish I had even a little hope. I cannot say forget me—but I would mention that there are impossibilities in the world.

Advice and criticism from her friends had continued to disturb her, and reading Keats's letter, she thought that once more he was anxious to forget her. But

> how could it ever have been my wish to forget you? [he wrote] how could I have said such a thing? The utmost stretch my mind has been capable of was to endeavour to forget you for your own sake

seeing what a chance there was of my remaining in a precarious state of health. . . . Believe too my Love that our friends think and speak for the best, and if their best is not our best it is not their fault.

In her note she promised that however long he was ill she would wait for him:

Then all we have to do [he answered] is to be patient. Whatever violence I may sometimes do myself by hinting at what would appear to any one but ourselves a matter of necessity, I do not think I could bear any approach of a thought of losing you.

It was not easy for either of them to be patient. Throughout February, though the doctors assured him that fine weather and peace of mind would restore his health, Keats felt ill and wretch-edly depressed. Fanny tried to hearten him, because it seemed wiser to be buoyant than tenderly sympathetic, and when her mother suggested that her written good-nights disturbed him, she sent him a note in a calmer, more sisterly tone. But she could not obey the orders of his doctors, the advice of Brown, the well-intentioned suggestions of her mother and still satisfy his own imperative needs; he had had long days and restless nights in which to brood, and, distressed by her behaviour, he answered with reserve:

My dear Fanny,
Do not let your mother suppose that you hurt me by writing at night. For some reason or other your last night's note was not so treasureable as former ones. I would fain that you call me *Love* still. To see you happy and in high spirits is a great consolation to me— still let me believe that you are not half so happy as my restoration would make you. I am nervous, I own, and may think myself worse than I really am; if so you must indulge me, and pamper with that sort of tenderness you have manifested towards me in different Letters. . . .

And then, his thoughts of fame, his old morbidity returning, he added:

"If I should die," said I to myself, "I have left no immortal work behind me—nothing to make my friends proud of my memory—

but I have lov'd the principle of beauty in all things, and if I had had time I would have made myself remember'd." Thoughts like these came very feebly whilst I was in health and every pulse beat for you— now you divide with this (may *I* say it?) "last infirmity of noble minds" all my reflection.

It was not the first time he had spoken to her of dying; but since July, when he had longed to possess death and Fanny together, she knew that his early death had become a proba⁄ bility. As she read this letter, her affected buoyancy and high spirits disappeared and she was yet again ill with apprehension. Her next note delighted him by its depth of feeling, but his reply, addressed to Mrs. Brawne, was given to Fanny at her mother's discretion:

> You spoke of having been unwell in your last note: have you recover'd? That note has been a great delight to me. . . . If I am to recover, the day of my recovery shall see me by your side from which nothing shall separate me. If well you are the only medicine that can keep me so. Perhaps, aye surely, I am writing in too depress'd a state of mind—ask your Mother to come and see me—she will bring you a better account than mine.

But Mrs. Brawne gave Fanny a tactful and encouraging ac⁄ count which carried no conviction. As Keats had recognized long ago, it was useless to try to deceive her, and she wrote to him now, asking for the truth.

> My dearest Girl,
> Indeed I will not deceive you with respect to my health. This is the fact as far as I know. I have been confined three weeks and am not yet well—this proves that there is something wrong about me which my constitution will either conquer or give way to. Let us hope for the best. Do you hear the Thrush singing over the field? . . .

It was now late in February; that Keats could hear Fanny's voice and occasionally see her in the garden made his long imprisonment less tolerable than ever. But he was "pretty well provided with Books," and his own were sent next door for Fanny's pleasure and comment, while she, who had few books of her own, lent him bound magazines; her mental companion, ship was a continual solace. Yet the careful optimism in his notes suggested the uncertainty of his health, and at times the very thought of her threatened to make him fevered. "He was long ill," wrote Brown, "and, at one period, unable to bear the presence of any one except his medical attendants and myself... I recollect his once saying—'If you would have me recover, flatter me with a hope of happiness when I shall be well; for I am now so weak that I can be flattered into hope.'" Brown, who waited on him day and night, still discouraged Fanny from coming and would try to keep her visits as brief as possible, while Keats himself, sick and suspicious, heard per, haps of Brown's valentine and resented his manner towards her, and told her not to "make any long stay with me when Mr. Brown is at home—whe[ne]ver he goes out you may bring your work."

In the pocket,book which Fanny kept during 1820 there are pencilled notes of "my lutestring body with scarlet," of "work unfinished: a muslin flounce for an apron ... my new morning gown," and a skein of silk which she must remember to buy. She never lost her interest in clothes, and in these February days, when she had watched Brown's bulky figure safely down the path, she would bring her sewing next door. It was now, as a token of her constancy, that she gave Keats a ring engraved with both their names:

My dearest Fanny,
    The power of your benediction is of not so weak a nature as to pass from the ring in four and twenty hours—it is like a sacred Chalice once consecrated and ever consecrate. I shall kiss your name and mine where your Lips have been—Lips! why should a poor prisoner as I am talk about such things. Thank God, though I hold them the dearest pleasures in the universe, I have a consolation

independent of them in the certainty of your affection. . . . Health
is my expected heaven and you are my Houri—this word I believe
is both singular and plural—if only plural, never mind—you are
a thousand of them.


But with February the expected heaven vanished. On
March 6th Keats had a violent heart attack. The doctor warned
Brown that a similar one might kill him.

Fanny possibly guessed the verdict from Brown's "wretched
depression" and the anxiety on her mother's face. She was told
that Keats could not even bear to receive a letter. For two days
he remained too weak to leave his bed, and troubled by the
slightest excitement, while both households lived in silent and
continual apprehension. On Wednesday a specialist in
respiratory diseases came from London to see him.

Dr. Bree, ignoring Keats's earlier bleeding from the lungs,
assured Brown that "there was no pulmonary affection, no
organic defect whatever—the disease is on his *mind*"; perhaps at
this stage Keats's body was indeed less stricken than his spirit,
for in the long silence which was forced upon him he learned
the pain which final separation would bring. Weak in body,
his spirit failing him, he longed more than ever to be flattered
into hope; and in the opinion of Dr. Bree and the solid assurance of Brown, who understood his needs, he tried willingly
to believe.

For many days Fanny remained at home, anxious to be near
him, hesitating to come downstairs if he rested in the front
room. Her notes were always as loving as he wished and spoke
of the walks she would take with him in the spring and
the travels they would enjoy together. Keats lay on his sofa
dreaming of their future and imagining her every movement
while she stayed next door. When she returned from a walk,
she would pass his window and fill him anew each time with
admiration: her beauty was enhanced by love and she wrote to

him that she sometimes feared he did not care for her so much as she desired.

> My dear Girl I love you ever and ever and without reserve [he answered]. . . . My Mind has been the most discontented and restless one that ever was put into a body too small for it. I never felt my Mind repose upon anything with complete and undistracted enjoy-ment—upon no person but you. . . . The anxiety shown about our Loves in your last note is an immense pleasure to me: however you must not suffer such speculations to molest you any more.

Fanny treasured his letters, and his comment on his restless mind and powerless small body sank into her mind, for when in middle age she told Medwin of Keats's illness, she sent him two lines of *Absalom and Achitophel*:

> The fiery soul, that working out its way,
> Fretted the pigmy body to decay.

"I never see those often quoted lines of Dryden," she wrote, "without thinking how exactly they applied to Keats."

Sometimes, during this long month, despite herself, she showed that she was tired and anxious: "You appear'd very much fatigued last night," he noticed, "you must look a little brighter this morning. I shall not suffer my little girl ever to be obscured like glass breath'd upon, but always bright as it is her *nature to*." He tried to encourage her and, perhaps, to raise his own spirits: "I rely upon taking a walk with you upon the first of May." But several times his palpitations returned; Fanny reluctantly kept her visits to certain days of the week, and though she would not ask him to stop writing to her, she begged him at least to compromise with his doctors and not to write too much.

At last it seemed as if his health were returning with the spring. His old ambition stirred, and he thought of poems and the "few fine plays" within his power to write:

> Let me have another op[p]ortunity of years before me and I will not die without being remember'd.

And whatever he might say in a burst of rhodomontade or a moment of depression, Fanny knew "that his most ardent desire was to live to redeem his name." The magnitude of his destiny she never doubted. Fiercely condemning the malignity of his critics and what she believed was indifference in his brother and his friends, she told Fanny Keats that he was made for immortality, "formed for every thing good, and, I think I dare say it, for every thing great."

Though March was nearly over she remained at Wentworth Place, not merely to hearten him by her passive presence but perhaps to ensure that in moments of grief or disappointment he did not again grow reckless of his health. She was afraid that he might become over-tired, and every day she asked for a detailed report of his progress. There were few moments when he was distant from her mind, and Keats himself would fill her briefest absence by writing to her:

> Though I shall see you in so short a time I cannot forbear sending you a few lines. You say I did not give you yesterday a minute account of my health. Today I have left off the Medicine which I took to keep the pulse down and I find I can do very well without it, which is a very favourable sign, as it shows that there is no inflam-mation remaining. You think I may be wearied at night you say: it is my best time; I am at my best about eight o'Clock. . . . How can you bear so long an imprisonment at Hampstead? I shall always remember it with all the gusto that a monopolizing carle should. I could build an Altar to you for it.

At last, when April had nearly come, she ended her im-prisonment; perhaps the spring demanded a visit to her dress-maker. Keats welcomed her home with new assurance and the happy officiousness of an invalid:

> As, from the last part of my note you must see how gratified I have been by your remaining at home, you might perhaps conceive that I was equally bias'd the other way by your going to Town. Though I am pleased with the one, I am not displeased with the other. How

do I dare to write in this manner about my pleasures and dis-
pleasures? I will tho' whilst I am an invalid, in spite of you. Good
night, Love!

His tone suggested that he was fast recovering, but his
cheerfulness was sometimes shadowed by a thought of Shakespeare's tragedy, the prescience that his own death might not
be worthy of Juliet; and there was "a great difference between
going off in warm blood like Romeo, and making one's exit
like a frog in a frost."

It was nearly a month since his first critical attack, yet at
times he was still too weak for Brown to allow him excitement.
His last letter to Fanny in March is a pitiful comment on his
condition:

> Dear Girl,
>   Yesterday you must have thought me worse than I really was.
> I assure you there was nothing but regret at being obliged to forego
> an embrace which has so many times been the highest gust of my
> Life.

On April 1st Keats told his sister that he grew better every
day, and that were it not for occasional faintness and difficulty
in breathing, he would think himself quite well; for the first
few days of the month he continued to improve, walking on the
Heath and venturing to London, and his physician recommended another walking tour. Keats knew the hardships of
such a life too well to accept the suggestion, but as Brown was
soon to let Wentworth Place for the summer, he was compelled
to think of leaving Hampstead, and in mid-April, too
troubled to speak of what lay close to his heart, he had to consider separation from Fanny.

The "horrid morbidity of Temperament" which he had long
since recognized as his most persistent enemy hung continually
upon him: and Fanny, anxious about his present condition,

became profoundly sad about the future. Her sorrow, if she showed it, served to increase his own, and her attempted gaiety wounded him; as the month advanced she felt ever-growing strain. She understood his mind: even Brown was persuaded that no one knew Keats better. But though her devotion remained, ill-health and advancing time made him morbidly possessive, and Mrs. Dilke, on a visit to the Brawnes, recorded her own anxiety and that of Fanny's mother: "It is quite a settled thing between John Keats and Miss Brawne. God help them. It's a bad thing for them. The mother says she cannot prevent it, and that her only hope is that it will go off. He don't like anyone to look at her or to speak to her." Keats, who could not bear "any approach of a thought" of losing Fanny, knew now that he was not barred from her by the summer alone.

## XI

◆◆◆

EARLY IN MAY he decided to move to Kentish Town until Brown returned. He was also planning his more distant future: "I have my choice of three things—or at least two—South America or Surgeon to an I[n]diaman—which last I think will be my fate—I shall resolve in a few days." We can only speculate on the third possibility which he abruptly dismissed, but perhaps for a moment of bitterness he rejected literature. On May 7th he sailed with Brown in the smack as far as Gravesend, and returned to his new lodging, 2, Wesleyan Place, Kentish Town; he had chosen to be near Hunt's house in Mortimer Terrace, for in Hunt's companionship he was ever happy.

His separation from Fanny was to be as long as possible, for he would be too disturbed if he bade her frequent farewells. His table was bright with buttercups and cowslips which she had given him, knowing that he loved wild flowers. She had made him promise to write and send her books, and the mental companionship of the early spring continued; he re-read his Spenser, again admiring the "sea-shouldering whales," marking lines for her and comforting himself in giving her happiness. "I have sent you Spenser," Fanny wrote to his sister, three years later, "which you will find the more pleasure in reading as you will find the best parts marked by one who I have heard called the best judge of poetry living—they were marked for me to read and I need not tell you with what pleasure I did so."

On May 15th Keats told Brown: "I am well enough to extract much more pleasure than pain out of the summer." He had been away from Wentworth Place for only a week. But as the separation lengthened, remembrance haunted him; his spirit was too weak to combat it, and by the end of the month his old morbidity and a new jealousy took possession.

His dying mother, the slow death of Tom and his own medical training had taught Keats to recognize, without hesitation, the insinuating progress of consumption. As early as 1817 he had taken mercury to improve his health, and long before the exertion of the Scottish tour he had seen the first signs of disease; on the tour itself he had written of spending a year in America "if I live to the completion of the three next." At Shanklin, longing for the luxury of death, he may have thought that he would know it soon; and now, wanting life, he was left brooding and alone, his apprehension confirmed. The autumn would not end his pain of mind, for his physicians, fearful of an English winter, had advised him to go to Italy. He lived old ecstasies again in torment and, with the fevered brain of a consumptive, magnified vexations to Sophoclean size: Fanny, laughing with her mother's guests, dancing at the Dilkes' party, smiling over the valentine from Brown. His books lost power to comfort and distract, his ring

became the symbol of her long unfaithfulness, and in his
suffering he wrote to her:[17]

> I am tormented day and night. They talk of my going to Italy. 'Tis
> certain I shall never recover if I am to be so long separate from you:
> yet with all this devotion to you I cannot persuade myself into any
> confidence of you. Past experience connected with the fact of my
> long separation from you gives me agonies which are scarcely to be
> talked of. When your mother comes I shall be very sudden and
> expert in asking her whether you have been to Mrs Dilke's, for
> she might say no to make me easy. I am literally worn to death, which
> seems my only recourse. I cannot forget what has pass'd. What?
> nothing with a man of the world, but to me dreadful. . . . When you
> were in the habit of flirting with Brown you would have left off,
> could your own heart have felt one half of one pang mine did.
> Brown is a good sort of Man—he did not know he was doing me to
> death by inches. I feel the effect of every one of those hours in my side
> now . . . and I will never see or speak to him until we are both old
> men, if we are to be. . . . I have heard you say that it was not unpleasant
> to wait a few years—you have amusements—your mind is away—you
> have not brooded over one idea as I have, and how should you?
> You are to me an object intensely desireable—the air I breathe in a
> room empty of you is unhealthy. I am not the same to you—no—you
> can wait—you have a thousand activities—you can be happy with
> out me. Any party, any thing to fill up the day has been enough.
> How have you pass'd this month? Who have you smil'd with? All
> this may seem savage in me. You do not feel as I do—you do not
> know what it is to love—one day you may—your time is not come. . . .
> I appeal to you by the blood of that Christ you believe in: Do not
> write to me if you have done anything this month which it would
> have pained me to have seen. You may have altered—if you have
> not—if you still behave in dancing rooms and other societies as I have
> seen you—I do not want to live—if you have done so I wish this
> coming night may be my last. I cannot live without you, and not
> only you but *chaste you; virtuous you.*

Fanny was living within two miles of him, more uncertain
than ever, after seventeen months' betrothal, if he would
marry her, and not knowing when or even if she would be with

him again. She had loved him in his long absence, in imposed conditions of secrecy, in his illness, in his moods which were not always easy to understand or forgive; when he was too ill to bear her presence she had given up her freedom only to be near him, and she would have done so now had he been at Wentworth Place. But that in his absence she should refrain from visiting her friends was more than any woman could grant; and that Keats not merely resented her small pleasures, but savagely denied her love and doubted her faithfulness hurt her profoundly.

Mrs. Brawne collected this letter when she went to see Keats; she admitted that Fanny had been alone to London. He wrote a second letter which increased Fanny's misery, for she saw that the careful convalescence of the spring had been undone:

> You could not step or move an eyelid but it would shoot to my heart—I am greedy of you. Do not think of any thing but me. Do not live as if I was not existing—Do not forget me—But have I any right to say you forget me? Perhaps you think of me all day. Have I any right to wish you to be unhappy for me? You would forgive me for wishing it, if you knew the extreme passion I have that you should love me—and for you to love me as I do you, you must think of no one but me. . . . Your going to town alone, when I heard of it was a shock to me—yet I expected it—*promise me you will not for some time, till I get better*. Promise me this and fill the paper full of the most endearing names. If you cannot do so with good will, do my Love tell me—say what you think—confess if your heart is too much fasten'd on the world. . . . Well may you exclaim, how selfish, how cruel, not to let me enjoy my youth! to wish me to be unhappy! You must be so if you love me—upon my Soul I can be contented with nothing else. If you could really what is call'd enjoy yourself at a Party—if you can smile in peoples faces, and wish them to admire you *now*, you never have nor ever will love me. I see *life* in nothing but the certainty of your Love—convince me of it my sweetest. If I am not somehow convinc'd I shall die of agony. If we love we must not live as other men and women do. . . . You must be mine to die upon the rack if I want you. . . . For God's sake save me—or tell me my passion is of too awful a nature for you.

Fanny probably received these letters together. In her misery she told him that he had ill-treated her in word, thought and deed. To his sister she wrote, after Keats's death: "You do not, you never can know how much he has suffered. So much that I do believe, were it in my power I would not bring him back."

On the morning of June 22nd, Keats spat a little blood; he spat it rather more copiously that night. His physician said there was no need for anxiety, but the following day Keats appears to have moved to Hunt's house in Mortimer Terrace. Hunt did all in his power for the comfort of his friend, trying to distract him from his unhappiness; but nothing could for a moment divert Keats from Fanny. He brooded over her every movement, her every change of countenance, and every word that she had uttered to him. To pronounce her name was impossible. He was afraid to see her, so great would be his pain in parting; but from his prison he kept his eyes "fixed on Hampstead all day."

"Seeing him once change countenance," wrote Hunt,[18] "in a manner more alarming than usual, I pressed him to let me know how he felt; upon which he said, that his feelings were almost more than he could bear, and that he feared for his senses. I proposed that we should take a coach and ride about the country together." Through the still lanes where the birds were faint with sun, they rode to Hampstead; they passed within a few yards of Wentworth Place and rested on a bench in Well Walk. The air was sultry with the scent of lime flowers and heavy with memories of Tom; and in his sick, unreasoning mind Keats doubted Fanny's love. He told Hunt, "with unaccustomed tears in his eyes that 'his heart was breaking.'" "Winding southwardly from the heath," remembered William Hone,[19] "there is a charming little grove in Well Walk, with a bench at the end; where I last saw poor Keats,

Tuesday Morn —

My dearest Girl,

I wrote a letter for you yesterday expecting to have seen your mother. I shall be selfish enough to send it though I know it may give you a little pain, because I wish you to see how unhappy I am for love of you, and endeavour as much as I can to entice you to give up your whole heart to me whose whole existence hangs upon you. You could not step or move an eyelid but it would shoot to my heart — I am greedy of you. Do not think of any thing but me. Do not live as if I was not existing — Do not forget me — But have I any right to say you forget me? Perhaps you think of me all day. Have I any right to wish you to be unhappy for me? You would forgive me for wishing it, if you knew the extreme passion I have that you should love me — and for you to love me as I do you, you must think of no one but me, much less write that sentence. Yesterday and this morning I have been haunted with a sweet vision

LETTER FROM KEATS TO FANNY BRAWNE

the poet of the 'Pot of Basil,' sitting and sobbing his dying breath into a handkerchief."

*Lamia, Isabella, the Eve of St. Agnes, and Other Poems* was published by Taylor and Hessey on July 1st. "I have been delighted with this volume," Severn wrote, "and think it will even please the Million"; of Keats's physical condition, however, he spoke with distress: "His appearance is shocking and now reminds me of poor Tom—and I have been inclined to think him in the same way—for himself—he makes sure of it—and seems preposse[ss]ed that he cannot recover." On July 12th Mrs. Gisborne "drank tea at Mr. Hunt's," and "was much pained by the sight of poor Keats under sentence of death from Dr. Lambe. He never spoke and looks emaciated." Soon afterwards, aware continually of his sentence, Keats received a letter from Wentworth Place: Fanny begged him not to leave her and she wanted to see him.

> My dearest Fanny,
> ... Upon my soul I have loved you to the extreme.... You complain of my illtreating you in word thought and deed—I am sorry,—at times I feel bitterly sorry that I ever made you unhappy—my excuse is that those words have been wrung from me by the sha[r]pness of my feelings.... I could give way to my repentant feelings now, I could recant all my suspicions, I could mingle with you heart and Soul though absent, were it not for some parts of your Letters. Do you suppose it possible I could ever leave you? You know what I think of myself and what of you. You know that I should feel how much it was my loss and how little yours. My friends laugh at you! I know some of them—when I know them all I shall never think of them again as friends or even acquaintance. My friends have behaved well to me in every instance but one, and there they have become tattlers, and inquisitors into my conduct: spying upon a secret I would rather die than share it with any body's confidence. ... People are revengeful —do not mind them—do nothing but love me. ... Your name never passes my Lips—do not let mine pass yours. ... After reading my Letter you even then wish to see me, I am strong enough to walk

over—but I dare not. I shall feel so much pain in parting with you again. My dearest love, I am affraid to see you, I am strong but not strong enough to see you. Will my arm be ever round you again. And if so shall I be obliged to leave you again. My sweet Love! I am happy whilst I believe your first Letter. Let me be but certain that you are mine heart and soul, and I could die more happily than I could otherwise live. . . . My fairest, my delicious, my angel Fanny! do not believe me such a vulgar fellow. I will be as patient in illness and as believing in Love as I am able.

Less unkind than those which she had already received, the letter troubled Fanny with its suspicion and secrecy. But about the time of her birthday Keats returned part of one of her notes, asking her to re-write it more lovingly. Still brooding over her correspondence and the past, the voyage to Italy and a brief, tormenting future, too sick in body and mind to express himself in poetry, and adding the term of endearment last, that no one else might see it, he wrote to her again. It was a cruel letter for her to receive:

If my health would bear it, I could write a Poem which I have in my head, which would be a consolation for people in such a situation as mine. I would show some one in Love as I am, with a person living in such Liberty as you do. Shakespeare always sums up matters in the most sovereign manner. Hamlet's heart was full of such Misery as mine is when he said to Ophelia "Go to a Nunnery, go, go!" Indeed I should like to give up the matter at once—I should like to die. I am sickened at the brute world which you are smiling with. I hate men and women more. I see nothing but thorns for the future—wherever I may be next winter in Italy or nowhere Brown will be living near you with his indecencies—I see no prospect of any rest. Suppose me in Rome—well, I should there see you as in a magic glass going to and from town at all hours,——I wish you could infuse a little confidence in human nature into my heart. I cannot muster any—the world is too brutal for me—I am glad there is such a thing as the grave—I am sure I shall never have any rest till I get there. . . . I wish I was either in your arms full of faith or that a Thunder bolt would strike me.

On Thursday, August 10th, Fanny's reply was brought to Mortimer Terrace. Keats was resting and Mrs. Hunt asked a servant to give it to him; but the servant, being under notice, gave the letter to Thornton Hunt, telling him not to show it until the following day; and on Saturday the child produced it. The letter contained, Mrs. Hunt told Mrs. Gisborne, "not a word of the least consequence." Keats, who held Fanny's name too sacred to be spoken, and who would rather have died than share the secret of his love, was given her opened note. "Poor Keats," Mrs. Gisborne recorded, "was affected by this inconceivable circumstance beyond what can be imagined; he wept for several hours, and resolved, notwithstanding Hunt's entreaties, to leave the house."

He said later that he had intended to return to his rooms in Well Walk; but there was no hope of health away from Fanny. That evening, for the last time, he returned to Wentworth Place.

## XII

AUTUMN WAS approaching and he could not now endure a rigorous English winter. He would have to leave for Italy within a month. It was the moment for the final decision which Fanny herself remained powerless to make. She had awaited it for nearly two years, through a few weeks of perfect happiness and many months of criticism, uncertainty and grief. Had the decision been hers alone, she would beyond doubt have chosen to marry Keats immediately. She was not yet of age, and the decision was made for her by her mother.

For a moment, to her, the marriage seemed imminent: perhaps Mrs. Brawne, entrusting the younger children to relations, would come to Italy, too. But Mrs. Brawne only promised that when Keats returned he should marry Fanny and live with them. "Most people said," remembered a neighbour,[20] "my mother amongst the rest, who was Fanny's great friend, that Mrs. Brawne was quite right to put an end to it, as Keats was not able to keep a wife, and his health was so bad he was not likely to return from Rome."

It was not only Mrs. Brawne who prevented the marriage: Keats himself, who had offered before to release Fanny from her betrothal, foresaw his future too certainly to marry her now.

The thought of the journey woke him at daylight every morning and haunted him "horribly. I shall endeavour to go though it be with the sensation of marching up against a Battery." The slightest exertion confirmed his foreboding, and he sent his publisher a testamentary paper.

He wrote a brief note to Hunt: "You will be glad to hear I am going to delay a little time at Mrs. Brawne's"; and Hunt replied: "You judge rightly . . . sick wisdom, I think, should love to live with arms about its waist." Hunt often came to Wentworth Place, and he found a new serenity in Keats's countenance and behaviour: "he was at times more than tranquil." Mrs. Brawne and Fanny nursed Keats devotedly; and later, in Italy, he remembered these "few happy days" as the only halcyon moments of his life, the only time when his mind had been at ease.

Yet, as August advanced, every movement that Fanny made, every phrase she uttered, sank into his mind, and throughout the month he tried to conceal his foreboding from her. He wrote to Brown asking him to come with him to Rome, confessing the frailty of his hopes and, perhaps, the depth of his passion. He would be introduced to a Dr. Clark in Rome, but there was a core of disease in him "not easy to pull out . . . I ought to be off at the end of this week, as the cold winds begin to blow towards evening;—but I will wait till I have your answer to this." Brown boarded a smack at Dundee and the wind was fair.

September came, the trees in the garden hung heavy, and the harvesters sat by the furrows in Hampstead fields. The mornings and evenings grew colder and the birds set out on their journey towards the sun.

On September 11th, to save him from exertion, Fanny wrote Keats's farewell to his sister: "It is not illness that prevents me from writing but as I am recommended to avoid every sort of fatigue I have accepted the assistance of a friend, who I have desired to write to you when I am gone and to communicate any intelligence she may hear of me. I am as well as I can expect and feel very impatient to get on board as the sea air is expected to be of great benefit to me. My present intention is to stay some time at Naples and then to proceed to Rome."

With Fanny's consent, he destroyed the letters she had sent him, though she kept his note from Hunt[21] and the letter from the Olliers regretting that they had published his first book of poetry. He had already given her Hunt's pocket-book, and *Foliage*, Spenser, the Dante he had taken to Scotland and in which Fanny had copied the sonnet she loved so well; and now, perhaps at parting, he offered her his copy of *The Cenci* and the treasured facsimile of the folio Shakespeare in which he had written his comments and the sonnet on *King Lear*. He gave her an Etruscan lamp, and his miniature, the perfect likeness which Severn had painted of him; and to Margaret he gave an amethyst brooch. Fanny gave him a new pocket-book, a paper-knife, and a lock of her hair, taking one of his own in exchange. She lined his travelling cap with silk, keeping some material in remembrance. She gave him, too, a final token, an oval white cornelian: it was a talisman to bring him courage, dispel his angry passions and evil thoughts, to preserve him from lightning and tempest, fever and enchantment.

On Wednesday, September 13th, 1820, she said good-bye to him. Her grief was past expression; she could only write in her diary: "Mr. Keats left Hampstead."

## XIII

❖❖❖

THE FOLLOWING Monday, Fanny heard that Keats and Severn
had sailed. She lost no time in sending the news to his sister.
She had long wanted to show her friendship to Fanny Keats,
and now it would be, for both of them, the greatest solace:

My dear Miss Keats,

Your brother on leaving England expressed a wish that I should
occasionally write to you; a wish with which I feel the greatest
pleasure in complying, but I cannot help thinking I require some
kind of introduction, instead of which I must inform you of all my
claims to your correspondence and I assure you I think them no
slight ones, for I have known your brother for two years, am a great
friend of Mrs Dilke's who I believe you like, and once sent you a
message, which I do not know whether you received by a lady who
had then never seen you but who expected to do so, a Mrs Cornish.
Besides which I have several times invited you to stay with me during
the last time your brother George was in England, an indulgence
which was not granted me. You see I have been quite intimate with
you, most likely without you ever having heard of my name. Besides
*all* this your brother has been staying with us for the last six weeks of
his being in this country and my Mother has nursed him. He left us
last Wednesday but as the ship waited a few days longer than we
expected, he did not sail from London till 7 o'clock yesterday morning. This afternoon we have received letters from two of his friends
who accompanied him as far as Gravesend; they both declare his
health and spirits to be better than they could have expected. . . . I
cannot tell you how much every one have exerted themselves for him,
nor how much he is liked, which is the more wonderful as he is the
last person to exert himself to gain people's friendship. I am certain
he has some spell that attaches them to him, or else he has fortunately
met with a set of friends that I did not believe could be found in
the world. May I hope, at some time to receive a letter from you?
Perhaps you have an objection to write to a stranger. If so, I will
try not to be very much disappointed if your objection is too strong
to be overcome. For my own part I have long ceased to consider you
a stranger.

Fanny Keats was a quiet, unspoiled girl of seventeen, kept under strict supervision in her guardian's house at Waltham, stow. She had waited impatiently for the letters and rare visits of her eldest brother, and now that he had sailed for Italy she readily accepted the eager affection of one who had known him. Fanny Brawne's letter began a friendship which lasted for years and proved to be not only comforting at the time, but of unexpected and permanent importance.

Among other members of his circle, however, Keats's departure did not rouse such kindly feeling; the Reynolds family, who had long been jealous of Fanny Brawne, hailed it as the end of her betrothal. "I am very, *very* much pleased," Reynolds wrote to Taylor, "and the more so, since Keats has departed so comfortably, so cheerfully, so sensibly. I cannot now but hold a hope of his refreshed health, which I confess his residence in England greatly discouraged, particularly as he was haunted by one or two heartless and *demented* people whose opinions and conduct could not but silently influence the bearings of his Thoughts & hopes. Absence from the poor idle Thing of woman-kind, to whom he has so unaccountably attached himself, will not be an ill thing." "I hear," Jane Reynolds wrote to Mrs. Dilke, "that Keats is going to Rome, which must please his friends on every account. I sincerely hope it will benefit his health, poor fellow. His mind and spirits must be bettered by it; and absence may probably weaken, if not break off, a connexion that has been a most unhappy one for him."

On September 28th, the *Maria Crowther*, blown by contrary winds, put into Portsmouth, and Keats and Severn visited the Snooks at Bedhampton. Mr. Snook found Keats much better than he had expected, yet Keats must have suffered wordless pain of spirit. His mind returned to the visit, nearly two years ago, made in the January of *St. Agnes' Eve*, and to Brown, when the ship had sailed, he expressed his unceasing agony:

Even if my body would recover of itself, this would prevent it. The very thing which I want to live most for will be a great occasion of my death. . . . I wish for death every day and night to deliver me from these pains, and then I wish death away, for death would destroy even those pains which are better than nothing. Land and Sea, weakness and decline are great seperators, but death is the great divorcer for ever. . . . I think without my mentioning it for my sake you would be a friend to Miss Brawne when I am dead. You think she has many faults—but, for my sake, think she has not one—if there is anything you can do for her by word or deed I know you will do it. . . . The thought of leaving Miss Brawne is beyond every, thing horrible—the sense of darkness coming over me—I eternally see her figure eternally vanishing. Some of the phrases she was in the habit of using during my last nursing at Wentworth place ring in my ears. Is there another Life? Shall I awake and find all this a dream? There must be we cannot be created for this sort of suffering.

And as the *Maria Crowther* lay off the Isle of Wight, he remembered how once, at Shanklin, he had prayed to her star "like a Hethen," longing to die, eternally in her embrace. Now, as he yearned unbearably for life, he knew that only within her arms had life been found; and in his copy of Shakespeare's Poems, opposite *A Lover's Complaint*, he wrote his own fare, well to life and poetry, a final version of the sonnet which Fanny had loved:

> Bright star! Would I were stedfast as thou art—
>   Not in lone splendor hung aloft the night
> And watching, with eternal lids apart,
>   Like nature's patient, sleepless Eremite,
> The moving waters at their priestlike task
>   Of pure ablution round earth's human shores,
> Or gazing on the new soft,fallen masque
>   Of snow upon the mountains and the moors.
> No—yet still stedfast, still unchangeable
>   Pillow'd upon my fair love's ripening breast,
> To feel for ever its soft swell and fall,
>   Awake for ever in a sweet unrest,
> Still, still to hear her tender,taken breath,
> And so live ever—or else swoon to death.

Early in October, through a letter sent to Mrs. Dilke, Fanny heard that Keats had been to Bedhampton, and that the voyage had already improved his health; but "I cannot say," she told Fanny Keats, "this news pleases me much, I was in hopes that by this time he was half-way to Naples."

Keats and Severn reached Naples on October 21st, as dawn was breaking. The white houses, rising tier upon tier on the hills, surrounded by green vineyards and dusky olive trees, were lit by the early sun; and the light struck the smoke clouds banked over Vesuvius. Keats seemed to lose himself in so much beauty. But he did not long enjoy his pleasure and absorption; the *Maria Crowther* remained in quarantine for ten days and no passengers were allowed to disembark. His thoughts ranged over Vesuvius, the vineyards, the white-sailed craft in the harbour, and returned within himself; Naples became the symbol of delights unshared and others not to be fulfilled, and Fanny receded ever further from him, into the other, lost world. He could not bring himself to write to her, but he wanted to assure her that he could not forget; and he wrote his first and only letter to her mother:

> My dear Mrs Brawne,
>
> . . . I dare not fix my Mind upon Fanny, I have not dared to think of her. The only comfort I have had that way has been in thinking for hours together of having the knife she gave me put in a silver-case —the hair in a Locket—and the Pocket Book in a gold net—Show her this. I dare say no more. . . . My Love again to Fanny—tell Tootts I wish I could pitch her a basket of grapes—and tell Sam the fellows catch here with a line a little fish much like an anchovy, pull them up fast. . . .
>
> Good bye Fanny! God bless you

Yet, as he himself had told her a few months earlier, he would never be able to bid her "an entire farewell." Waiting in Naples harbour, he thought of her continually, and of her alone.

Bright Star, would I were stedfast as thou art—
Not in lone splendor hung aloft the night.
And watching, with eternal lids apart,
Like nature's patient, sleepless Eremite,
The moving waters at their priestlike task
Of pure ablution round earth's human shores,
Or gazing on the new soft-fallen masque
Of snow upon the mountains and the moors.
No—yet still stedfast, still unchangeable
Pillow'd upon my fair love's ripening breast,
To feel for ever its soft swell and fall,
Awake for ever in a sweet unrest,
Still, still to hear her tender-taken breath
And so live ever—or else swoon to death.

BRIGHT STAR SONNET BY KEATS

. . . The persuasion that I shall see her no more will kill me. I cannot q[uit]. My dear Brown, I should have had her when I was in health, and I should have remained well. I can bear to die—I cannot bear to leave her. O, God! God! God! Everything I have in my trunks that reminds me of her goes through me like a spear. The silk lining she put in my travelling cap scalds my head. My imagination is horribly vivid about her—I see her—I hear her. There is nothing in the world of sufficient interest to divert me from her a moment. . . . O that I could be buried near where she lives! I am afraid to write to her—to receive a letter from her—to see her handwriting would break my heart—even to hear of her anyhow, to see her name written, would be more than I can bear. My dear Brown, what am I to do? Where can I look for consolation or ease? If I had any chance of recovery, this passion would kill me. Indeed, through the whole of my illness, both at your house and at Kentish Town, this fever has never ceased wearing me out. When you write to me, which you will do immediately, write to Rome (*poste restante*) —if she is well and happy, put a mark thus +; if—

My dear Brown, for my sake, be her advocate for ever. . . . I am afraid to write to her—I should like her to know that I do not forget her. Oh, Brown, I have coals of fire in my breast. It surprises me that the human heart is capable of containing and bearing so much misery. Was I born for this end? God bless her, and her mother, and my sister, and George, and his wife, and you, and all! . . .

Far away, in Louisville, George himself had been thinking of Fanny and early in November he sent Keats some advice: "Marriage might do you good." He added: "If we meet a safe opportunity for England we will send Miss Brawn an india Crape dress or merino shawl or something scarce with you, but cheap with us. She has our thanks for her kindness during your illness." The letter,[22] posted to Hampstead, was opened by Brown. He never sent it to Italy.

In her second letter from Fanny Keats, Fanny Brawne had received a warning: Mrs. Abbey disapproved of her writing to Walthamstow, and the arrival of two letters from Hampstead within a short time would have made her both inquisitive and unpleasant. "I should write a eulogium on that lady's character," Fanny Brawne declared, "but that I am affraid of some unlucky accident which might expose at the same time my opinion and our correspondence. Even now I tremble at what I have said as I am ignorant whether you receive your letters in public or whether you have private arrangements for that purpose." At the end of November she broke her prudent silence of more than seven weeks:

> We received a letter from your brother about a fortnight ago. So I dare say did you. I was so extremely happy to hear of his arrival at Naples, that I overlooked the hardships of their wretched voyage and even the bad spirits he wrote in. The weather was so much against him, joined to his spirits, which prey on him and continually make him worse, that it would have been too much to expect any great improvement in his health.

On the first day of December, Brown heard from Keats. The letter "quite weighed him down." Soon afterwards one from Severn was forwarded to him; Severn had been "horror struck" and moved to tears by Keats's suffering: "If I can but cure his mind I will bring him back to England—*well*—but I fear it can never be done in this world."

Brown read the letter to the Brawnes, "skipping & adding, without the slightest suspicion on their part," telling Fanny that if Keats's spirits improved, Severn expected an early recovery. It was the first illusion which, well-meaning but unkind, he had tried to give her, and Fanny eagerly accepted it. She wrote at once to Walthamstow:

> My dear Girl
>   Mr. Brown has received a letter from [Mr. Keats]. When he wrote they were just arrived on shore, their sufferings during the quarantine were beyond any thing we can imagine. From your brother I never expect a very good account, but you may imagine how lowering to the spirits it must have been when Mr Severn who I never imagined it was possible for any thing to make unhappy, who I never saw for ten minutes serious, says he was so overcome that he was obliged to

relieve himself by shedding tears. He however says your brother was a little recovered. He says, if he can but get his spirits good, he will answer for his being well in a moderate time, which shows he does not consider he has any complaint of consequence.

Just before Christmas, however, Brown received a letter from Keats. It "put him to the torture," and not for two days did he mention it to Fanny. Keats had said that writing and even reading increased his pain, that the thought of past happiness was enough to kill him. Brown told Fanny that Keats felt as well as he could expect, and would write again soon. But the letter did not come. Christmas passed and the new year began.

Early in January Brown heard that Keats had had a relapse, and that there was small chance of his recovery. He had cried: "This day shall be my last!" and Severn had removed every means of suicide from his reach, fearful that he might destroy himself. It was now, wrote Severn, the ninth day of his relapse, he suffered continually, racked by physical pain and a thousand images in his memory and imagination; that he could again become his former self seemed beyond hope.

Brown told Mrs. Brawne at once. She was "greatly agitated," and decided that henceforward Fanny must not know the worst. She intimated, gently, that the news was grave. Fanny bore it "with great firmness—mournfully but without affecta-tion," and knowing the meaning of her mother's kindness, she answered only: "I believe he must soon die, when you hear of his death, tell me immediately—I am not a fool." "Poor girl!" Brown wrote to Severn, "she does not know how desolate her heart will be when she learns there is no hope, and how wrtched she will feel—without being a fool . . . you and I well know poor Keats desease is in the mind—he is dying broken-hearted . . . take care you do not open a letter with *my* hand-writing on the address which *contains another* handwriting— there is such a letter, and you can avoid opening it by peeping inside." The letter arrived in Rome in mid-February, and Severn gave it to Keats, supposing it to come from Brown. Keats glanced at it; his pain was past description, and the effects remained upon him for many days. He could not read it but asked Severn to bury it with him.

It was mid-January, four months since he had left Went-worth Place. Both households lived in continual and growing apprehension. Upon Fanny the strain had become intolerable. Despite Mrs. Brawne's reassurance, she knew for certain what she had long since feared. She was compelled to hide her increasing anxiety; she could not confide in her mother, who had never fully understood her love, nor in her friends, who were either disapproving or indifferent, and she felt that, as long as possible, Fanny Keats should be spared unhappiness. "When Mr. Severn wrote," she told her, "they were in Rome. They lodged opposite an English Physician to whom they were recommended, and who paid them the greatest attention. Your brother went out on horseback every day. I am extremely glad they have chosen Rome instead of Naples for their winter residence. I am sure the climate is far preferable." But Fanny could not indefinitely hide her feelings now:

> Do, my dear Girl, if you have any intelligence of them, let me know it, however trifling we shall feel it of the greatest consequence. The time is so long before either party can receive letters, that it makes me very impatient.

Towards the end of the month Brown heard "that there was no hope and no fear of a lingering illness. Miss Brawne," he wrote to Severn, "does not actually know there is no hope, she looks more sad every day. She has insisted on writing to him by this post, take care of the letter—if too late, let it be returned un-opened (together with the one with *my* hand-writing on the address and *her's* inside) to *Mrs.* Brawne."

On February 1st Mrs. Brawne had a letter from Severn; he said he still firmly believed that Keats might return. Yet the very hope of Keats's recovery lay in his new tranquillity, and he was tranquil because he no longer wished to live. Fanny wrote that day to Walthamstow. She had controlled her anxiety for nearly five months; it could no longer be restrained:

My dear Girl

I have been this week wishing to write to you but putting it off every day in hopes of having something concerning your brother to communicate which would not give you pain, but it is in vain to wait any longer. Oh my dear, he is very ill, he has been so ever since the 8th of December. If I had written this letter two hours sooner I should have owned to you that I had scarcely a hope remaining and even now when I have just received a letter from Mr. Severn with the nearest approaching to good news that we have had since this last attack, there is nothing to rest upon, merely a hope, a chance. But I will tell you all in as collected a way as I can. On the 10th of Jan^ry Mr Brown received a letter from Rome saying your brother had been attacked with spitting of blood and that the symptoms were very bad. He had been ill for 17 days and did not appear to get better. I judged of you by myself and though I was then about to write I deferred it for some time in hopes a letter more cheering might arrive. I cannot think I was wrong. If you knew how much I regretted that it had not been kept from me—how continually I thought a fortnight or even a weeks ignorance of it would have been more pain spared—and when at last I could not bear to keep silence any longer for fear you should fancy the least neglect should have occasioned it, I wrote a letter that without mentioning anything bad, did not, if I may judge from your answer, give you hopes of a speedy recovery. Once or twice we have heard slight accounts, which were neither calcu-lated to raise or depress our hopes but yesterday I was told of a letter from the Physician which said he was exactly the same. He did not get better nor did he get worse. But could I conceal from myself that with him, not getting better was getting worse? If ever I gave up hope, I gave it up then. I tried to destroy it, I tried to persuade myself that I should never see him again. I felt that you ought no longer to remain in ignorance and the whole of this day I have been thinking how I could tell you. I am glad, very glad, I waited, for I have just received the account I spoke of in the beginning of this letter. Mr Severn says that for the first time he feels a hope, he thinks he shall bring him back to us. Surely, that is saying a great deal— and yet the reason he gives for that hope destroys it, for the last 3 days (the letter was dated the 11th of Jan) your brother had been calm, he had resigned himself to die. Oh can you bear to think of it, he has given up even wishing to live—Good God! is it to be borne that he, formed for every thing good, and, I think I dare say it, for every thing great, is to give up his hopes of life and happiness, so young too, and to be murdered, for that is the case, by the mere malignity of the world, joined to want of feeling in those who ought above all to have felt for him—I am sure nothing during his long illness has hurt me so much as to hear he was resigned to die. . . .

And now my dear Girl, my dear Sister for so I feel you to be, for- give me if I have not sufficiently softened this wretched news. Indeed I am not now able to contrive words that would appear less harsh— If I am to lose him I lose every thing and then you, after my Mother will be the only person I shall feel interest or attachment for—I feel that I love his sister as my own—God bless you.

Mrs. Brawne, in her mistaken kindness, still withheld the gravest news, but she felt the strain of silence and of her daughter's grief:

Your letter afforded me great consolation [she answered Severn] if it were only hearing Mr Keats was in a tranquil state of mind how much I feel for you how unfortunate his being out of England or happy shou'd I have been to have assisted you in nursing him after the distressing accounts we have heard I scarcely dare have a hope of his recovery but I will trust to what you say When you talk of bringing him to England it cheers us for believe me I shou'd consider it among the happiest moments of my life to see him in better health

On February 17th Taylor heard from Severn: the con- tents of his letter were again withheld from Fanny. Keats was suffering indescribably. The doctor said that he should

never have left England, for even then he had been in-
curable; the journey had shortened his life and increased his
pain.

In Italy the fruit trees had been long in blossom, and Severn
had tried to comfort him with thoughts of spring. It was the
season Keats loved best, and he would not know it again. Bitterly he wept. "He kept continually in his hand a polished, oval,
white cornelian, the gift of his widowing love, and at times it
seemed his only consolation, the only thing left him in this
world clearly tangible."

Monday Morn
[February 26]

My dear Fanny,

 I enclose you the letter I promised you but I cannot send with it
any news that would give you pleasure. A letter has been received,
which I have not seen dated the 25th he was not worse but he was
not better, and faint as are the hopes Mr Severn gives I dare not
think them well founded. All I do is to persuade myself, I shall
never see him again—but I will not say any more perhaps it may
afford you more comfort to hope for the best. God bless you my
dearest girl in a week or a fortnight I will write to you again unless
I hear from Italy, should that be the case you shall be immediately
informed of it.

March came, and Mrs. Brawne heard again from Severn:
the hope of death had become Keats's only comfort. The
letter was not shown to Fanny, "from whom the worst is kept
back," wrote Brown, "in (to my mind) a very ill-judged way.
Meanwhile she fears perhaps worse than is supposed." In
vivacity or silence she still tried to hide her feelings. Sometimes her boisterous gaiety surprised him; sometimes she
seemed to sink under apprehension. On March 9th he told
Severn: "Mrs. Brawne sends her remembrance to you—Miss
Brawne said not a word, and looked so incapable of speaking, that I regretted having mentioned my writing to you
before her."

Monday Morn

My dear Fanny

I enclose you the
letter I promised you but I cannot
send with it any news that would give
you pleasure. a letter has been
received, which I have not seen
dated the 25th. he was not worse
but he was not better, and faint
as are the hopes. Mr Severn gives

LETTER FROM FANNY BRAWNE TO
FANNY KEATS

Late on Saturday, March 17th, the news reached Went-worth Place. On Friday, February 23rd, a little before midnight, Keats had died in Severn's arms.

> I felt at the moment utterly unprepared for it [Brown wrote to Severn]. Then *she*—she was to have it told her, and the worst had been concealed from her knowledge ever since your December letter. It is now five days since she heard it. I shall not speak of the first shock, nor of the following days,—it is enough she is now pretty well,—and thro'out she has shown a firmness of mind which I little expected from one so young, and under such a load of grief.

# The Years After
## 1821-1865

### I
❖❖❖

THE BRAWNES went into mourning, and now, for the first
time, Fanny's betrothal was made evident. Alone, her hair cut
short, and wearing the ring which Keats had given her, the
cap and black dress of a widow, she wandered across the
Heath, day after day; often, retracing their walks, she stayed
there far into the night, until some watchman, bearing his
lantern, at last discovered her.[1]

Wentworth Place, all Hampstead seemed a perpetual
symbol of past happiness. Now and suddenly she felt the
aftermath of passion, indefinite absence, violent letters and the
prolonged anxieties of Keats's illness and long-awaited death;
and her own suffering "nearly cost her her life."[2] Reticent as
she had always been, she kept her emotions to herself; her
mother would hardly understand them, and Samuel and
Margaret were too young to understand. But the little girl of
eleven "carried into advanced life the recollection that, when
the stress of keeping up appearances passed, Fanny spent such
time as she remained at home in her own room—into which
the child would peer with awe, and see the unwedded widow
poring in helpless despair over Keats's letters."[3] Fanny grew
"alarmingly thin,"[4] all colour left her face, her brown hair
faded; and when, the following year, *The Fortunes of Nigel*
appeared, a neighbour[5] wondered if Scott, who often heard
Hampstead gossip, had drawn her likeness in Lady Hermione:
"I was very ill . . . my recovery was long doubtful. . . . My

health was restored at length, against my own expectation and that of all around me. But when I first again beheld the reflec-tion of my own face, I thought it was the visage of a ghost."

One person only, whom Fanny had never seen, could understand her grief. Nine days after hearing the news, she brought herself to write to his sister:

> You will forgive me, I am sure, my dear Fanny, that I did not write to you before, I could not for my own sake and I would not for yours. . . I should like to hear that you my dearest Sister are well, for myself, I am patient, resigned, very resigned. I know my Keats is happy, happier a thousand times than he could have been here, for Fanny, you do not, you never can know how much he has suffered. So much that I do believe, were it in my power I would not bring him back. All that grieves me now is that I was not with him, and so near it as I was. Some day my dear girl I will tell you the reason and give you additional cause to hate those who should have been his friends, and yet it was a great deal through his kindness for me for he foresaw what would happen, he at least was never deceived about his complaint, though the Doctors were ignorant and unfeeling enough to send him to that wretched country to die, for it is now known that his recovery was impossible before he left us, and he might have died here with so many friends to soothe him and me *me* with him. All we have to console ourselves with is the great joy he felt that all his misfortunes were at an end. At the very last he said "I am dying thank God the time is come", and in a letter from Mr Severn written about a fortnight before he died and which was not shown me, so that I thought he would live months at least if he did not recover he says . . . "We now dare not perceive any improve-ment for the hope of death seems his only comfort" . . . The truth is I cannot very well go on at present with this, another time I will tell you more. . . . And now my dear I must hope you will favor me with your company, it will I assure you be a real favor. . . . Fix your own time my dear, only come . . . we will do as much as we can to amuse you and to prevent your thinking of any thing to make you unhappy . . . you are the only person in the world I wish to see.

A few days later, afraid as she was of Abbey, Mrs. Brawne prevailed on herself to visit Fanny Keats in Pancras Lane.

Mrs. Dilke went with her "to give her courage," and they asked Mrs. Abbey if the young girl might stay for a little while in Hampstead. Mrs. Dilke, impetuous and anxious to strengthen her case, confided to Mrs. Abbey the secret of Keats's betrothal, but Mrs. Abbey manifested little surprise. She promised, however, that Fanny Keats should visit Wentworth Place, and Mrs. Brawne went home with satisfaction. Her triumph was short-lived, for Mrs. Abbey withdrew her promise, and the lonely girl stayed on at Walthamstow.

April brought no happiness to Wentworth Place. The new-leaved trees, the green world beyond the hedge, the returning swallows, and the full-throated nightingale singing towards evening in the quiet garden seemed but a reminiscence of another spring. A letter from Severn to Taylor reached Hampstead about April 16th, and Fanny learned how the Italian health authorities had burned the furniture in Keats's room, scraped the walls and made new windows and doors and floor. She read of the post mortem and the funeral near the monument of Caius Cestius, and how Dr. Clark had made the men plant daisies on the grave, saying that Keats would have wished it. Unknown to her family, slowly and with great pain, she copied the account of his last days; she did not seal it because his sister might want to read it, but she herself could not look at it again. Bitterly lonely, and needing consolation, she sought it now where Keats himself had found it. Reading the folio he had known so well, she came next day to the end of *As You Like It*, and pencilled beside the word 'Finis' her own name and the date: "Fanny April 17 1821."

The first three weeks of May she spent in London, where Mrs. Dilke entertained her, trying to keep her mind from returning to the past. Fanny remained pale and grew thin throughout the spring, though in the presence of friends she expressed no unhappiness. Her love of Keats lay too deep for

casual conversation;. with his sister alone, whom she wished
"more than ever" to see, she would discuss him:

> To no one but you would I mention him [she wrote to Fanny
> Keats]. I will suffer no one but you to speak to me of him. They are
> too uninterested in him to have any right to mention what is to you &
> me, so great a loss. . . . Dear Fanny, no one but you can feel with me
> —All his friends have forgotten him, they have got over the first
> shock, and that with them is all. They think I have done the same,
> which I do not wonder at, for I [have] taken care never to trouble
> them with any feelings of mine, but I can tell you who next to me
> (I must say *next* to me) loved him best, that I have not got over it
> and never shall.

## II

SPRING PASSED and summer came, and still Fanny Keats
remained at Walthamstow; Mr. Abbey was deaf to her timid
entreaties, and Mrs. Abbey, afraid of his brusque, overbearing
manner, would not against his wishes allow the girl more
freedom. If Fanny Brawne did summon her courage and call
on him herself, she could not "persuade him to any thing," and
in June she began to organize help for what she called "the
cause." Caroline Robinson,* the "downright Miss" whom
Keats had so disliked, Mr. Abbey's neighbours and even the
neighbours' business acquaintances were enlisted: Mrs.
Cornish,* possibly the wife of an accountant known to Abbey
in the City; Bella Goss,* whose husband had served with him
on the vestry at Walthamstow; Mrs. Whitehurst,* whose
husband worked near Goss in the same tiny street off Queenhithe; Miss Rowcroft,* who had good reason to know the
Whitehursts, for her father had tried his hand at most of the
nautical trades. "How little we know what we may one day
come to," Fanny reflected in June: "If any one could have told
me, a year ago that I should ever be angling for Mr Abbeys
good opinion, I should have been surprized."

The campaign began successfully: Miss Robinson "offered her services and is almost," wrote Fanny, "as much interested in the cause as I am." Miss Robinson was soon taken to call on Mrs. Cornish, who by the greatest good fortune was about to go to Walthamstow. Fanny promptly gave her a "pressing invitation" to Hampstead, and in case that should prove insufficient Miss Robinson "promised to bring her some evening to drink tea. . . . And now my dear," Fanny Brawne continued, "make the most of her if you see her. I am told she is very good natured. Of course we must be careful not to let her know our reasons for courting her so much. . . . Miss Robinson . . . is very intimate with Mrs Whitehurst and I have no doubt will mention it to her, but Miss Rowcroft I believe knows Mrs Goss and perhaps you can make some use of her name. . . . God bless you my dearest girl. . . . Tell me when you write what is Mrs Abbey's opinion of Mrs Cornish."

Mrs. Abbey's opinion has not come down to us. The host of friends and neighbours vanish from Fanny's letters; but they seem to have served their purpose. Though Fanny Keats may not have come to Hampstead, by the autumn even Abbey's persistence wore down and Fanny Brawne went to Waltham-stow.

Walthamstow, "a large and populous village, including the hamlets of Clay Street, Marsh Street, &c.," lay "upon the borders of Epping Forest, to the left of the high road from London." It abounded, according to *The General Ambulator*, "with the villas of opulent merchants and tradesmen"; and, as another writer pointed out, the "country seats, farm houses and cottages, are so blended together, and the paths encompassed with trees and hedges, are so delightful, that no surprise can be manifested that so many opulent and respectable families reside on this healthy spot." The most opulent inhabitants in the early nineteenth century were Sir Robert Wigram and those of his twenty-two children who lived at Walthamstow House; among the most respectable were John Goss and his family, the Abbeys, the Lancasters, and (probably from Kilburn) a certain Thomas Brawne.

To this genteel and perhaps familiar village Fanny Brawne took the coach in September 1821. The combined diplomacy of Mrs. Cornish, Mrs. Goss, Miss Robinson, Miss Rowcroft and the Whitehursts had achieved its well-deserved and long-awaited triumph. One can hardly imagine her tumultuous feelings as she walked down the long and straggling hamlet of Marsh Street, past Miss Caley's where Fanny Keats had been to school, past the house in which the Goss family lived, and came within sight of Pindars. She passed the two-acre field and the well-stocked orchard, the garden stretching far down to the canal, and reached at last the large house itself.

Richard Abbey proved to be stout and benevolent-looking, opposed to progress and fond of antiquated clothes; his wife's appearance was also surprising, for Fanny had "expected a more portly red-faced dame. She is much more in the motherly nursry style." On this wet September day Mrs. Abbey received her kindly, showing indeed such concern about thin shoes and damp feet that Fanny grew suspicious: perhaps Mrs. Abbey was merely unwilling to let her ward out of the house. But whatever her motive, and despite Fanny's boast that she "never on any occasion caught cold," Mrs. Abbey refused to allow them to walk in the fields. Within Pindars' four walls Fanny Brawne first conversed with Keats's sister.

For a year and more she had longed to share with Fanny Keats a thousand small memories which the world would not understand, to recognize a familiar look or a mannerism; and the younger girl, who had yearned to break her silence, talked happily of the days at Edmonton, her brother's pleasure "in keeping fish (called minnows I think) and his love of birds, especially a favourite Tom Tit." They spoke abundantly and eagerly, delighting or grieving at every detail which came to mind, rejoicing in each other's company; and Fanny Keats promised that when in October she came to Pancras Lane they would meet again. It was in a slightly chastened mood that Fanny Brawne wrote to remind her; for, despite her boast to Mrs. Abbey that she was immune from colds, she had "a very disfiguring one."

In the same letter a close friend of the Brawnes made his first appearance: it was Valentine Maria Llanos y Gutierrez, "lean, silent, dusky and literary," who had spoken to Keats three days before he died; by the time Fanny's letter reached Pindars he was staying with the Wigrams in Walthamstow and he had already seen Keats's sister.

> Guiterez dined with us yesterday [Fanny wrote some time later] and told me he had seen an acquaintance of mine. After guessing for an hour to no purpose, for though I thought of you it seemed so im' probable I did not mention it, my Mother found out; of course we laughed at him finely for his polite offer of calling on you. How' ever I informed him your guardian is particular and cautioned him against letting the family see you are acquainted. Don Valentine Maria Llanos Guiterez is a pretty name, is it not? he himself is everything that a Spanish Cavalier ought to be. You need not be affraid of speaking to him for he is extremely gentlemanly and well behaved.

Fanny Keats answered, confessing perhaps what she later confessed to George: she thought that Valentine Llanos was "handsome, elegant and graceful in his manners and deport' ment, accomplished and possessed of considerable talent," and she could safely say "that under the canopy of heaven there does not exist a nobler minded or purer hearted being." Her thoughts were also occupied with literature, for she continued to receive parcels of books from Wentworth Place and tried to improve Mrs. Abbey's taste in reading as well as her own. But "I don't at all think," remarked Fanny Brawne, "you will succeed in making Mrs Abby a literary lady."

In the November weather Fanny remained at Hampstead, reading widely. She sent Samuel to Pancras Lane with a note for Abbey's ward, only to learn that Fanny Keats was not expected for a week. Wentworth Place remained silent and unvisited, nor did she care for any society; her solitude was merely broken by a visit to the Dilkes: "There I heard only one thing to please me, [Mrs. Dilke] has quarrelled, I hope for ever with the Reynolds. My dear Fanny if you live [to] the age of the Methuselem and I die tomorrow never be intimate with the Reynolds." They belonged, as she had long since known, to the coterie who had tried to take Keats from her.

Throughout the winter she was heartened by a deep and growing friendship. Fanny Keats, who was three years younger than herself, had left school early and against her will, and ever since she had been deprived of the company of books and people; to Fanny Brawne she must have seemed remarkably immature. But she had, none the less, a touch of Keats's character: a sense of humour, a love of nature, an eager interest in books, a willingness to learn. She was ready enough to borrow books and discuss them, and volumes of *The Indicator*, *The London Magazine*, Byron, Spenser and, it seems, French literature, were sent to and fro by the carrier, who was "as good as a footman." Fanny herself delighted in sharing with Keats's sister a little of the literary companionship which she had once known with him. "I wish I knew what books you have read," she complained, "for I would write about them, there is nothing I like better to talk about." "Don't you or do you admire Don Juan? . . . I think Beppo nearly as good. . . . When you read it you will notice that gratifying account of us English young ladies—I believe I did not tell you that Donna Inez was in- tended for Lady Byron. . . . The character is beautiful and I

have no doubt very like for I have heard Lady B. is a blue-
stocking."

She had appointed herself Fanny Keats's literary guide, for
the young girl had once confessed her entire ignorance of
Shakespeare; she became her dramatic critic: "You did not see
Kean to the best advantage [in *King Lear*] and the play itself
is spoiled." When Fanny Keats grew afraid of the effect of
opium, Fanny Brawne turned mentor. She discussed George
Keats, who was "more blamed than he should be," and
William Ewing, "so fluttered and confused," who dined with
Brown and admired the Severn miniature. As for Valentine
Llanos ("I keep that name for best, and in common call him
Guiterez"), even if he called when everyone was out, or looked
undistinguished and more French than Spanish, his every visit
was recorded for Fanny Keats's pleasure.

The more she knew Fanny Brawne, the more the girl at
Walthamstow chafed at her own tedious and restricted life and
counted the months until she would come of age. Mrs. Abbey
insisted that she was seventeen, but Fanny herself knew that she
was older and wrote anxiously to Hampstead asking for a
birth certificate. Samuel was promptly sent to London to
procure one, but the result was sad: "You will find by the
register I enclose that you are but 18, for which I am very
sorry."

Christmas drew near: it would be the third anniversary of
the betrothal, the first since Keats had died. It appeared an
ironic season of happiness. To Keats's sister Fanny sent the
bound volume of *The Indicator* which she herself could not open
for emotion; from every page his spirit seemed to rise. She had
once copied the Hermes Sonnet in the Dante which he had
given her: she could not read it now; and *La Belle Dame Sans
Merci* moved her beyond expression.

The Brawnes, and probably Brown, would dine with the

Dilkes on Christmas Day; the circle seemed poignantly in, complete. The occasion would be "like most people's Christmas day's melancholy enough. What must yours be?" she wrote to Fanny Keats, "I ask that question in no exultation. I cannot think it will be much worse than mine for I have to remember that three years ago was the happiest day I had ever then spent."

It was ten months since Keats had died. She sent his sister two curls of her hair: one was dark, the other, cut off within the last year, was faded and light brown, "as different as possible." "I was at a party last night," she confessed to Fanny Keats, "the first *real* party I have been to this year—You would have laughed had you seen me dressed out in my cap &c—I did feel a little queer."

## III

◆◆◆

SEVERN WAS still in Italy, haunted by the memory of Keats. He had inquired more than once after Fanny; he had learned from Brown of her bitter mourning, her resolute self-control, her sad change of appearance and, at last, of her slow-returning tranquillity. Often he went to the Borghese Palace to gaze at the Titian face whose wide-set eyes, small mouth and brown, abundant hair, resembled hers so strangely and so strongly.[6] Several times he had almost written to her, but he had found no words; and now, after a year, it seemed that some token would better express his feelings.

"I have some hair of our poor Keats," he wrote to Brown on the first day of 1822, "and have been waiting for a friend to bring it to London. I have thought of a little conceit as a present to poor Miss Brawne—to make a Broach in form of my Greek Lyre, and make the strings of poor Keats's hair, but I cannot find any workman to do it." The half-strung lyre, the symbol of promise unfulfilled, was part of his design for Keats's tomb, and Brown understood that Fanny would find more sorrow than pleasure in the gift: the brooch was made, an exquisite golden lyre, strung with the poet's hair, but Severn gave it to his own daughter on her wedding day, forty years later.[7]

His kind intention would indeed have brought pain to Fanny Brawne. Indignantly she rejected the suggestion that she was lonely, but she remained, always, profoundly sad. Mrs. Brawne tried to keep her company: her kindly but endless conversation brought unsympathetic replies; Mrs. Dilke entertained, and benevolent friends invited Fanny to tea. But Keats's sister and one other woman whose name remains unknown were the only friends whom Fanny wanted to see. As she had learned to do, long ago, she withdrew into herself, living the past again in her strong imagination and in surroundings of oppressive reality.

"How *very* delightful it would be," she wrote to Fanny Keats, "to have you with me tonight, I am quite alone. I am always glad to get my *'family'* out (to provoke me they scarcely ever go) and then highly favored indeed is the person I would wish for or even admit. There is one and only one person in the world besides yourself that I would admit tonight and her coming is about as possible as yours. So you see you *are* highly favored—I was asked out to tea by some friends who thought I must feel *'lonely'*—for my part I think people are all mad." It was February 3rd; tomorrow she and Samuel would go to the theatre, walking to London and back on a wintry night. Their allowance was not yet due and they could not afford to ride, though the fare was only a shilling from Oxford Street.

Fanny had recently seen the recipient of her letter. It had been an eventful meeting. Mrs. Abbey, shrewdly enough, had asked about Valentine Llanos, and Fanny Keats, long counselled by Fanny Brawne, had played the *ingénue*: "How I liked that sly question," wrote Fanny Brawne, "about Mr Guiterez that morning. I did not dare look up for fear of laughing but it

amused me to see how people commit themselves by trying to
see through others. I felt so glad I had told you because I
thought it must have delighted you as it did me. It was quite a
scene."

Though the Abbeys' disapproval made every meeting
difficult, she saw Fanny Keats again within the next few
weeks. In her three-hour visits (and each was "a visitation, in
Mrs. A.'s opinion"), she had already planned a future for
Keats's sister; in two years' time, when the young girl came of
age, they were to live together at Wentworth Place. To Fanny
Keats, imprisoned by the Abbeys, any thought of marriage
was an impractical dream; and to Fanny Brawne marriage
remained impossible. In dress and spirit she was wedded to
remembrance, and there seemed no happier future than to live
with Keats's sister in the house which he had known.

Having expressed their strong disapproval of her engagement, her relations now grew anxious for her welfare, and in
March her aunt, Mrs. Gould, invited her to Hampton for a fortnight, enticing her with promises of a visit to Hampton Court.
It was, however, with mixed feelings that Fanny wrote
announcing her departure:

> In a day or two I am going out for a few days and when I return I
> shall be so much engaged that I shall not call in Pancras lane for
> some weeks; which I do not regret for I dare say Mrs Abby makes
> herself more disagreeable than usual whenever you have any of your
> friends to see you. What an uncomfortable way we are obliged to
> see each other in. Two years seems a long while to look forward,
> yet I do look forward to the end of that time and think with the
> greatest pleasure how different our acquaintance (I don't like the
> word friendship) will be then, at least I hope so, and I am sure if you
> feel as well disposed towards it as I do, we shall be very happy
> together. One thing you can do, which is, to let me know if you go
> to any public places, exhibitions &c. There I should feel more at my
> ease with you than in any house belonging to Mr Abbey. . . . One of
> the places I am going to is Hampton Court. I would give the world
> if you could go with me the palace is so beautiful.

Hampton retained its air of pleasant gentility, dignified, perhaps, by the residence of the Duke of Clarence and copious Fitzclarences at Bushey Park; the Misses Walpole lived, by royal bounty, at Hampton Court, adding a nominal lustre to society; and to be listed like John Gould among the nobility and gentry of Hampton was not without its advantages. Elegant social life continued throughout the week, and on Sundays, for social or devotional reasons, the gentry attended the parish church, "an inconvenient and very old building, by no means corresponding with the high respectability of the neighbourhood; the walls of its interior," adds a contemporary, "are nearly covered with monuments." The neighbourhood was adorned with "many beautiful seats," while Moulsey Hurst, across the river, was "often the scene of pugilistic contests"; it was entertaining to watch the optimistic anglers on the bank, the carriages and horses crossing the Thames by ferry, and Hampton Court had retained its perpetual fascination. At Hampton Fanny remained, not a fortnight, but nearly five weeks.

She returned to London early in May to stay with the Dilkes in Great Smith Street, and Mrs. Brawne, who had lost track of her movements, welcomed her home with surprise on the evening of May 6th. A letter had been waiting for some time at Wentworth Place, in which Fanny Keats had offered her some tame pigeons. As her favourite cat had been lost during her absence, she could accept them safely, and this she did next day

> with the greatest pleasure, they come at a very good time . . . you must give me directions [she wrote] how to keep them and whether I am to get them a house. I hope they will stay with me. . . . You must tell me if they are to be kept indoors or out—We have no out-houses nothing but a tool house—Will they, if let out, join other pigeons and leave me? I ask these questions because I should be sorry to lose them through my inexperience. I mean to read what Buffon says of pigeons, tonight.
>
> I have read Buffon but he gives me no account how I am to feed them, so I must rely entirely on you.

The pigeons arrived: Primrose, Mary and Trutken. Fanny sent birds in exchange by the carrier. But Primrose fell victim to the cats, and soon there were too many bachelors and widowers: "Do," urged Fanny, "if you have a hen pigeon to spare let me have it, but I would rather go without unless you can be *certain* it is a hen. Perhaps you may have one that is a widow—by cats &c. . . . I would not have any more but I have so many that have no wives." The pigeons were no passing fancy, for two years later she was still guiding their matrimonial affairs: she had a new dragon runt, "a husband for one of my single ladies but the other is such a beauty (they call her a dragon pouter) that I shall wait till I can marry her more to my satisfaction."

Though Fanny had missed only one opportunity, she had seen all too little of Fanny Keats during the winter. She was always ready "early enough" to set out for Pancras Lane, she arrived, one can be sure, as the clock was striking: but her visits were never long enough, and though she invariably stayed for three hours she wanted to stay for six. Abbey re-mained a bigoted disciplinarian and she was still compelled to organize casual meetings in London; "Now I think of it per-haps we shall meet at the exhibition in about ten days . . . if, when you go, you can give me a tolerable long notice, I think I can meet you there."

Fanny Keats had been reading de Quincey; she displayed some curiosity about Byron's life. Under the tutelage of Fanny Brawne she was showing, too, all the lazy absorption of a reader. "I hope you will not," wrote her tutor, somewhat reproachfully, "from my asking for the two books, hurry with the rest for you are perfectly welcome to them for years . . . nobody returns a Pamphlet or newspaper—under nine months." But though Keats's sister was not yet a literary critic ("what little of your books you *can* read you never tell me a word about"), she had long ago become the elder girl's dearest companion:

"Oh Fanny I wish to goodness you were two or three years older—I get quite disheartened when I think of it. . . . I have been very comfortable at Hampton. There is a palace there built by Cardinal Wolsey, a great part of it filled with pictures, I went over it several times and made a vow to myself—that as soon as you were free from your present slavery I would take you down to see it. . . . God bless you, dear Fanny."

The summer of 1822 passed uneventfully, marked only, it seems, by a visit to the Dilkes or a call from Valentine Llanos: "Mr. Guiterez' brother," learned Fanny Keats, "is gone to join the independents in South America rather odd that, to fight against his own country." Braving Abbey, and that "worthless old woman," his wife, Fanny Brawne went again to Pancras Lane. The literature flowed on between Hampstead and Walthamstow, despite the pupil's misgivings and the tutor's occasional censorship: "The postman did not cheat you about the papers, I find they must be put in at Lombard Street to go free. . . . I shall miss one week's paper as it is not a very proper one—I want to send you a magazine and a volume of Shakespeare, how shall I get them to you?"[8] Fanny herself was reading about the care of birds, and growing anxious as the pigeons were nesting again.

The day before her birthday she returned to Hampton to stay with her aunt for three weeks; and when she confessed that she had seen only one palace in her life, Mrs. Gould took her to Windsor. They drove through Eton where Fanny's cousin, Beau Brummell, the Buck as his fellow pupils had called him, had been to school more than thirty years ago. Above the huddle of red, unequal roofs the white majestic castle rose in the summer sun, and as Fanny approached the gates she hoped, in vain, to see the King; but George IV was on board the *Royal George* on his way to Scotland.

None the less, the holiday ended in excitement, for a cogent

letter arrived from Margaret: Mr. Romay,* the Spanish music
master, was about to leave Hampstead. Such was the force of
the note that on August 29th Fanny reurned to Wentworth
Place. She found that Brown had left for Italy, and her sister's
message was confirmed. She had to break the news to Fanny
Keats, whose interest in the guitar, and indeed in everything
Spanish, grew daily more intense:

> My dear Fanny
>
> I left Hampton last thursday summoned to town by a letter from
> Margaret to the following effect. "Dear Fanny, for heaven's sake come
> home directly, Mr Romay leaves Hampstead on the 8th for Brussels"
> —This was nearly the whole of her letter and you may conceive the
> effect, every day seemed an age untill I could set to town. Alas, it
> is too true that he leaves Hampstead next sunday, but there is a
> chance of their going to Guernsey instead of Brussels and I do not
> think they will leave London immediately, but did you ever know
> any thing more wretched? Our hopes of comfort are at an end. You
> may take leave of the guitar. When you write to me I shall expect
> to hear that you are in despair.

But the desperation of Fanny Keats was mitigated by an
offer to take her to Hampton Court in the autumn, and some
sisterly advice on wearing white silk at dances; for however
Mr. Romay might disappoint her, Mr. Abbey had been persuaded to relax his rules. And such was his sudden generosity
that from his famous garden at Walthamstow, in which
every currant-bunch had once been counted, he had sent
Mrs. Brawne a melon, "a very fine one."

Consternation reigned at Wentworth Place: the Romays'
departure had been postponed, but they might be coming on
Sunday to take their leave. If Fanny Keats could spend the
week-end in Hampstead, she would see them once again, but
an aunt had arrived and seemed likely to occupy the spare bed:

> I really am [wrote Fanny Brawne] so teized by different things I
> scarcely know what I am doing. I have destroyed your letter. . . .

I wanted to ask you to come here tomorrow night, and I would if I could, go to town with you on Monday morning. . . . The reason I want you to come is that the Romay's leave town next wednesday, and they may come out on sunday, though I know nothing about it as I am now expecting them, but in consequence of a horrible train of mistakes which have nearly driven me mad, I am much affraid they will not come—You must come if my Aunt is gone. The Abbeys cannot think it strange of your coming for so short a time if however I am prevented from seeing you the best dress maker I know is Mrs Bell,* 62 Newman Street—Oxford Street. . . . My Mother thinks my Aunt will stay plague take it but I shall write again—

If the promised letter was written, it has not been preserved and the fate of the Romays, and of Fanny Keats's guitar, is unfortunately unknown.

There came other events, however, to occupy Fanny Brawne: her dog was ill and bit her hand and the doctor so bandaged it that she could hardly write. The housemaid took charge of the pigeons and they did not prosper:

> I am quite in despair about my pigeons [Fanny wrote to Waltham-stow]. I believe they are the most refractory pair in the kingdom— they never lay more than one egg and never make anything of that . . . about a week back they laid one which untill last night they sat on with great care, but this morning it was found pushed out of the nest. . . . It is supposed they must have had a matrimonial quarrel in the middle of the night for a great scream was heard at that time by my Mother from one of them after which all was quiet—Now in applying to you to know whether you can account for it I am taking counsel's opinion on the subject so pray give it with all due gravity.

From Walthamstow came advice about the pigeons and anxious inquiries about Fanny's hand; but visitors and the "sloppy weather" which she so disliked prevented her from answering in person. The story of Carlo's misdeed, however, which had been grossly enlarged, had by now alarmed her younger relations, and she replied to Fanny Keats with some amusement:

> Perhaps you will fancy, as my cousins did, that a terrible operation was performed, my hand dissected and half-carried away and a most delightfully horrible story it was, but unfortunately for those who delight in these wonders I had only a little caustic applied, which is nothing at all to talk about.

## IV

FANNY HAS recorded little about herself in the early months of 1823, except that she visited Fanny Keats in Pancras Lane and the Dilkes in Westminster. Neighbours in Hampstead met her at Roberts', the bakers in Downshire Hill, or at Gowland's, the grocers in New End; she would collect her books from a library in the High Street, and post her letters nearby in the box at Mrs. Eleanor Lovell's, pausing to admire the bright painted toys in the window. Sometimes she would be accompanied by Margaret, who was fourteen and unusually lovely, or by Samuel, a pale, thin, brown-haired boy with a Brummell interest in fashion; she herself still wore her widow's clothes. It was no mere display, for even now she could not open the Spenser which Keats, in his suffering at Kentish Town, had marked for her.

She lent the book indefinitely to his sister, and offered to give her "the serious poems of Lord Byron . . . as my dear Keats did not admire Lord Byrons poetry as many people do, it soon lost its value with me." She sent her, too, the *London Magazine* which contained the review of *Endymion*; "the articles called table talk are very good—they are by Mr Hazlitt—those signed Elia are considered very beautiful. . . . In this I give your dear brother's opinion as far as I could get it now." Keats had delighted in lending her his books, but his guidance had wrought more than he knew: she had come to share with Fanny Keats the conversations at Elm Cottage and Wentworth Place, the long and eager discussions across the Heath, the companionship of "one who I have heard called the best judge of poetry living."

In March and the following months she was often away from Hampstead: visiting the Rowcrofts, perhaps, in Upper Thames Street, Caroline Robinson, the Dilkes, and the Goulds again at Hampton. She went several times to Hampton Court, admiring the formal garden bright with tulips, and the peacock trees, memorials of the topiarist's art; she marvelled at the vast Tudor kitchens, and the dynasties emblazoned on the windows in the banqueting hall. She imagined the splendid extravagant court of Henry VIII and, having read Miss Aikin's book, the court of Elizabeth, while the Italian and Flemish masters and the portraits of Stuart kings roused her delighted admiration; her manifold pleasures were enhanced by the remembrance that in a year's time Fanny Keats could share them.

> I passed a pleasant time at Hampton [she wrote to her in July], and saw my old favorite Hampton Court several times. I hope to take you there yet, only a twelvemonth, Fanny, from last June. You had better begin Mrs Abbey's veil soon or she will never have it, bye the bye I have learnt some stitches for that sort of work and if you like I will show them to you.

Where Fanny spent her twenty-third birthday, indeed where she passed the late summer and early autumn remains unknown; two at least of her letters to Fanny Keats have not been preserved. In the late autumn she left Hampstead for a few days and stayed away a fortnight, probably with the Dilkes. Mrs. Dilke had changed little in the five years Fanny had known her: she remained vivacious, impetuous, well-meaning and anxious to introduce the repressed young woman into wider society.

In Fanny's own circle, however, there was some activity: since the day when Mr. Rowcroft had helped "to defray the expences of cloathing, &c. for the Spanish Army," the Row/ crofts had taken an interest in Iberian affairs; the eldest son had died "in the service of the Independents, near the Spanish Main," and now Miss Rowcroft announced her intention of going to South America, and was only deterred by inflamma/ tion of the lungs. She may have saved herself an untimely end, for her father, who became the British Consul in Peru, was soon shot dead by one of Bolivar's sentries on the Lima road. A more fortunate reminder of Spain was Valentine Llanos, who was now established in Hampstead society, and might already have been described as "an intimate friend of Mrs. Brawne"; so assiduous was he in his visits to Wentworth Place that perhaps he felt more than friendship for Mrs. Brawne's elder daughter. But for his marriage Fanny held and encouraged other hopes: "I met the Lancasters," she told Fanny Keats, "at a quadrille party at the Davenports—I think Miss Lancaster plain and *very* common and ungenteel looking. Mr Guiterez was there, the beau of the room."

But William Lancaster,* who lived in Marsh Street, not far from the Abbeys, was among the rich *élite* of Walthamstow. He had long been established in the City, and despite the demands of his fourteen other children, he could have provided a handsome dowry for his eldest daughter, Mary. Fanny Keats was understandably alarmed. Since Mr. Romay's departure she had abandoned the guitar and eagerly read *Don Quixote* and Spanish poetry; and now her literary achievements paled beside Miss Lancaster's social graces. Mary might be plain but she could afford to dress well, and Fanny needed reassurance from Wentworth Place.

> Don't alarm yourself [answered Fanny Brawne], about Miss Lan/ caster's appearance, I trust you would cut a better figure than she did. You might feel shy at first (which is not that I know of her failing) but any person of sense who goes out a little can soon get over that. . . .

It was February, and the year of Fanny Keats's independence, but Mrs. Abbey still clung to the reins of authority, grudging her meetings and insisting that she returned for dinner at "the unconscionable hour of half past two—Did I ever," asked Fanny Brawne, "think to hear of people dining at such a time in a christian country." But such difficulties did not deter her from calling at Pancras Lane, and Mrs. Brawne, too, went to London to inquire after Fanny Keats: she "saw the coachman and sent her compliments which I think it probable he kept for his own benefit."

Fanny Keats had not sent a letter for some time: she was still reading Spanish poetry. She remained uneasy about Miss Lancaster and wrote to George, asking him hopefully if she had a Spanish face; with the candour of elder brothers, he replied: "Your face is decidedly not Spanish, but English all over."

Fanny Brawne herself was fully occupied. It was probably now that she studied a small book "designed for the benefit of those who are unacquainted with the French and Italian languages," and learned Italian with determination; and on the fly-leaf of the *Nouveau Manuel du Voyageur*[9] she made calcula-tions of pfennigs and lists of cities on the Continent. She learned how to make common compliments and how to inquire after a person's health:

"What was your complaint?"

"A pleurisy followed by a putrid fever which brought me within an inch of the grave."

"You must be very cautious for some time to come."

"I am so. I eat nothing but little thin broths."

Perhaps it was now that she wrote short stories, translated from the German, and first thought of contributing to *Black-wood's*. In "Maga," said her son, years later, she published several tales, and one of her stories, printed elsewhere, may yet be traced by the couplet from Thackeray which precedes it; but one manuscript alone has survived: *Nickel List and His Merry Men, or, Germany in the 17th Century*.[10] It fills more than twenty-eight sheets of paper torn from a note-book, and seems to be a fair copy. Nickel List, as his surname implies, is a cunning robber: indeed he confesses "having been engaged in forty-nine principal robberies, besides innumerable smaller depredations." The story of his adventures, accompanied by footnotes, is fluent and carefully translated, but despite the bloodshed and continual violence, tedious it remains. The translator, however, who included *Frankenstein* in her book list, and preserved in her scrapbook the most ghoulish, fantastic cartoons, was not averse to the grim or the grotesque. Fanny turned with relief from unadventurous life to the seventeenth-century turbulence of *Nickel List*, "and a most delightfully horrible story it was."

Yet, though she may have retained her pleasure in Gothic horror, in literature, fashion and travel, during the last three years her character had noticeably changed. The gaiety which, in her letters, heartened Fanny Keats, was not always easy to maintain; her worn appearance suggested her inner loneliness, and she, who had been "very fond of admiration" and had received it so often at the Hampstead and Woolwich balls, was now indifferent to society. Miss Rowcroft's brother came to beg her to write to his sister, and Mrs. Dilke was, so Fanny thought, "quite affronted" by her silence.

> Can it indeed [she asked Fanny Keats] be four months since I wrote to you? I am certain you must possess the most forgiving disposition in the world to write to me after such neglect. Except that I ought to be and generally am, more careful in remembering you, than any one else, I could assure you that you are by no means the only person towards whom I deserve to be ashamed of my behaviour . . . you have been untill very lately the only person excepted from my general inattention. [She added]: I have not forgotten that the 18th of June is your birthday.

It seems strange that Fanny Brawne, who for several years had longed for the young girl to come of age, should not have remembered the date of her twenty-first birthday. Fanny Keats gained her independence on June 3rd. She was not completely happy, for Abbey had lost money in the City and she was anxious about her own capital in his charge; but soon after her birthday, hopefully planning her future, she wrote to Wentworth Place and asked for the names of quadrilles. Fanny Brawne recommended Musard's seventeenth set from the *Gazza Ladra* and Hart's seventh set from *Pietro l'Eremite*: she had an evident preference for Rossini. "You are now at liberty," she wrote, "and may do as you like, and I hope one of the first things you do will be to come and see me . . . this much I must say that nothing would give me so much pleasure."

# V
◆◆◆

IT WAS SOME little time before Fanny Keats left Walthamstow, but when she first came to stay at Wentworth Place, she seemed, after long years, to have returned to her family. The elderly woman who had loved Keats as a son accepted the young and uncared-for girl, his sister, as a child of her own. For the last four years Mrs. Brawne had deeply wished that she and her family had gone with Keats to Italy, she had thought with regret of every small kindness unperformed; and on his sister she now lavished all the motherly attention of which she was capable. This generous sympathy, the companionship of Samuel and Margaret, and, above all, the affection of Fanny, warmed and delighted the heart of Fanny Keats. She went with Fanny to Westminster and discovered the majesty of Hampton Court and Windsor Castle; she wandered, with Fanny, over the Heath which Keats had loved so well, and "O there is nothing like fine weather, and health, and Books, and a fine

country, and a contented Mind, and Diligent habit of reading
and thinking," and parties for dinner, for cards and quadrille.
To George she wrote praising the kindness of the Brawnes and
attesting the devotion of Fanny to herself and to Keats's
memory:

> I am very much gratified [answered George][11] to hear that Miss
> Brawne is an amiable Girl and that eccentricity has deceived my
> informants into the belief that she is unworthy, few things could give
> me more pleasure than to hear that the Lady of my dear Friend and
> Brother John's choice should be worthy of him. I trust I shall never
> forget Mrs. and Miss B.'s devoted attention to him during his
> sickness, their kindness to you encreases my debt;

and asking his sister "to forward a copy of Shelley's 'Adonais
*An Elegy on John*,'" he presented his respects "to Mrs. and Miss
Brawne, and say I should be most happy to hear from the latter
if it is only to give me a description of her present self, and
you. . . . I presume her sister is now a full blown Beauty."

Mrs. Brawne, who still "mingled in musical and literary
society," willingly entertained for Fanny Keats, and Valentine
Llanos came, confident in the future of his novel, and brought
with him a tall, adventurous young Irishman.

Gerald Griffin's career, like his appearance, was romantically
attractive: he had abandoned medicine for literature and come
to London with a few pounds and two tragedies, living at
times in poverty. This rejected but determined young writer,
whose career in some respects repeated that of Keats himself, discussed Keats with the poet's sister and Fanny Brawne. There
seems a touch of fiction in his account, for they told him, so
he recorded in June 1825, that they had often surprised Keats
with the *Quarterly* review in his hand, "reading as if he would
devour it—completely absorbed—absent and drinking it in like
mortal poison." But Fanny Keats saw little of her brother after
the review had appeared, and it seems unlikely that he would
have read it frequently at Walthamstow; Fanny Brawne wrote

later that she had seen nothing in his manner "to give the idea
that he was brooding over any secret grief or disappointment."
Of Fanny herself Griffin wrote to his sister: "Keats you must
know was in love, and the lady whom he was to have married
. . . is a beautiful young creature, but now wasted away to a
skeleton, and will follow him shortly, I believe."

His sad impression was shared by a small girl in Hampstead
who often came to have lessons from Margaret.[12] Years later,
though it was distorted by age and gossip, she drew her portrait of Fanny:[13] "She was a tall, handsome woman when I
first knew her, and must have been very beautiful before the
illness which robbed her of her colour. The illness followed the
breaking off of her engagement with Keats. . . . I am sure that
Fanny loved him and mourned bitterly for his death. I
remember her dark eyes and abundant light brown hair, but
expecially the extreme pallor of her complexion." Mrs.
Perrins added, to placate Victorian readers, that she would be
sorry "for lovers of Keats to think that the lady of his choice
was anything but a refined and cultured gentlewoman. In
every way she was well fitted to mate with him." But to this
vigorous old lady, despite some evident snobbery and inaccuracies, posterity should be grateful; she defended Fanny Brawne
from all too common misunderstanding.

In the summer of 1825 Fanny perceived that one of her
oldest and most cherished hopes would soon be fulfilled: that
all Fanny Keats's reading of Spanish poetry, her struggles with
the guitar, her anxiety to look Iberian, would at last, and
imminently, be rewarded. For the last few years she had advised
and encouraged her, and shared her confidence; and just as
Fanny Brawne's diplomacy had taken her to Walthamstow, so,
one feels, it had helped to bring Valentine Llanos to Hampstead. With her warm approval, he proposed to Keats's sister.

In accepting him she accepted the literary circles in which he

moved, and he gained a wife with a fortune, it is said, of some
£4,500.[14] On March 30th, 1826, they were married at
St. Luke's, Chelsea. They probably passed the early summer
in St. Marylebone, and in July Gerald Griffin spent "a very
pleasant evening" with them and "the intended bride of Keats,
as beautiful, elegant and accomplished a girl as any—or more
so than any I have seen here." At the beginning of August, the
Llanos went to France.

It seems likely that, before he left, Valentine introduced the
Brawnes to a young and distinguished diplomat at the Brazilian
Legation. João Antonio Pereira da Cunha,* who was to
become, some years later, the husband of Margaret Brawne,
had been in London since May; and in October, at the
remarkably early age of twenty-four, he was accredited
Brazilian chargé d'affaires. Margaret was already known for
her beauty, but the son of the Marquis de Inhambupé* would
have satisfied Mrs. Brawne's most fervent aspirations.

Fanny was past twenty-six, and remained in black for Keats,
discouraging any hopes which acquaintances might have
cherished. Not until 1827 was the Nestor of Hampstead, Dr.
Lord,* told that Fanny Brawne had just come out of mourning.[15] She had borne the signs of her widowhood for six years.

# VI

✦✦✦

FANNY BRAWNE remains, at about this time, an elusive
person, recorded only by the usual observant little girl.[16] Rosa
Rodd, who became Mrs. Perrins, was allowed as a concession
to stay up for her godfather's "grand fancy dress ball." In his
fine house at the Heath end of Well Walk there had gathered
Hampstead society, an assembly of Lalla Rookhs, Georgian
courtiers and Robin Hood's Merry Men: "The tall Dr. Lord
went as Little John," remembered Rosa Rodd, "Miss Brawne

(Keats's lady love) was also there, but I forget her dress. I went as a flower girl, with my nurse to look after me. A gentleman unfortunately offered me a shilling for a bunch of my flowers, which so delighted me that I afterwards sold the whole . . . the result of my grand mercantile speculations was my being sent home to bed." Fanny's comment on the occasion has not come down to us. At another ball, however, she met John Hamilton Reynolds, and their liking for one another had evidently not increased. Fanny's dress was liberally decorated with bugles: "It's good to wear bugles," Reynolds said, "and be heard wherever one goes." "And it's good to be a brother-in-law of Tom Hood's and get jokes for nothing," she answered. Her repartee, as usual, circulated in Hampstead.

But her brief year of bright clothes and gayer society was not to last much longer. Samuel had always been delicate, and had recently shown signs of consumption which Mrs. Brawne had seen in her sister and probably in her husband—that same disease from which Keats himself had died. At the beginning of 1828 Samuel's condition worsened rapidly:[17] "Poor Sam Brawne," wrote Dilke to George Keats, some time in March, "is as bad as he can be living. I went out to see him just before I left town and it seemed to me impossible that he would hold out a month." On the morning of March 28th, leaving his room for a moment, Mrs. Brawne returned to find him dead. Next day a short notice appeared in *The Times*, and on April 5th he was buried at St. Martin-in-the-Fields. He was twenty-three.

From childhood Fanny had been devoted to her one surviving brother. She was closer to him in age than she was to Margaret; he had been her frequent companion, sharing her interest in clothes and the theatre, her love of life: of all the family, he seems to have been most like her. His sudden and premature death brought her yet further suffering, and her distress was observed months later in her saddened face.

Not until the autumn did some happiness return to the family: William Steil, who had occupied Brown's half of the house, left Wentworth Place, and by September Valentine and his wife, with their one-year-old daughter, Irene, had returned from the Continent and come to live next door. To Fanny their companionship meant more than it had ever done. She welcomed Keats's sister and the small girl, while Valentine entertained her with descriptions of his travels. Barry Cornwall came to Hampstead and she met Patrick MacDowell.

Within a few weeks of his marriage, Valentine had copied her miniature of Keats, and talked of commissioning a sculptor to make a bust; in all probability he was thinking of MacDowell, who that year exhibited, in the Academy, two busts of "a Spanish gentleman." On the Llanos's return from their travels, Fanny was introduced to him, and in September, under her supervision and that of the poet's sister, the bust was finished. It seems to have caught the ardour of Keats's being, his latent, eager power.

Early in the new year an established friend of both families dined again at Hampstead. The tall figure of Gerald Griffin, his "expressive features and his profusion of dark hair, thrown back from a fine forehead, gave an impression of a person remarkably handsome and interesting." He spoke vividly of his travels in Ireland, his parliamentary reporting, his admiration for Joanna Baillie's plays and his study of law at London University; he had just begun research into ancient Irish history. Perhaps he recited some of his light verse about the theatre, deriding the appearance of "fat Chester" on the stage: it would have been a piquant comment on the future tenant of Wentworth Place.

Both Fanny and Margaret were of the company, and the conversation sparkled:

> My dearest Lucy [Griffin wrote to his sister], the other day. . . . I
> met that Miss B—— of whom I spoke to you some time since—sadly

changed and worn, I thought, but still most animated—lively and
even witty in conversation. She quite dazzled me in spite of her pale
looks. Her sister was there, younger and prettier, but not so clever.
If I were certain that the whole article were equal to the specimen
given, how I should wish that my dear Lucy had such a friend and
companion in her solitude! and how I should pity poor Keats!

Despite the brilliance of Fanny's conversation one feels her
inner weariness. She had spent the greater part of her eight
years' mourning in a house of memories. Her moments of
happiness with Keats had been exquisite; and now, as she wore
his hair in a locket at her neck, and the gold and almandine
ring which he had given her, she felt not only his benediction
but her unforgotten grief. Fanny Llanos, delighting in a small
daughter, expected another child in the summer; Margaret was
renowned for her loveliness, and perhaps even now received
tributes from a chargé d'affaires in Prussia; Fanny herself could
see happiness only in the past, and she was nearly twenty-
nine.

Yet, however her face had altered, posterity may see that her
belief in elegance remained. A French *émigré*, living in Oxford
Street, was cutting silhouettes at five shillings a full-length
portrait, three-and-sixpence if the sitter were under eight, and
only a shilling for a profile bust. So solid was the fame of
Augustin Edouart that the entire Stock Exchange sat to him
for their portraits and he earned the title of silhouettist to the
Royal Family of France and to the Duke of Gloucester.
Children, butlers, music masters, military and naval officers,
Miss Anna Fellowes, herb-strewer to King George IV, even
Mr. Sadler, Chief of Police in Cheltenham, flocked to Edouart
for their likenesses to be taken. From January to June 1829 he
worked in London, and during that time he cut a silhouette of
Fanny Brawne. The likeness may well be dated more precisely,
for on May 20th he portrayed another member of the small
Hampstead circle: "Master S. Garratt, Esq., Hampstead

SILHOUETTE OF FANNY BRAWNE
MADE IN 1829

Heath"; and probably Mr. Garratt, a future Queen's Counsellor, had shown Fanny the silhouette of his son.

Her own portrait is a full-length profile; there is strong character in her nose and chin, her tall cap adds to her height and to her graceful posture, and, holding a fan, she exemplifies the dress, manner and carriage in which she so firmly believed. Her family considered that the silhouette was characteristic and accurate as far as such things could be.[18]

Louis Mariano, the Llanos's son, was born in July. Whether Fanny was in Hampstead at the time of the birth is doubtful, for she stayed with Mrs. Gould in Bruges during the summer. It was her first recorded visit to the Continent, and she exercised her fluent French and German with delight, appreciated the strange, high-gabled houses and the Gothic church of Notre-Dame and its marble statue of the Virgin and Child, sculpted, it was said, by Michelangelo; and as she awoke in Bruges on her twenty-ninth birthday, she heard the bells of the old market hall chiming an ancient hymn.

In October, represented by her attorney, she was admitted tenant of the cottage at Twyford as the eldest sister of the late Samuel Brawne. It is stated,[19] though unconfirmed, that he had left her £800; it seems more likely that she had inherited half his share of the younger John Ricketts' estate. But before the end of 1829 she became a woman of considerable property, for within two years of losing her brother she suffered an even heavier bereavement.

Mrs. Brawne had never fully recovered from the shock of Samuel's death, and since August, perhaps for some time longer, she had suffered from a physical disorder. On October 29th she made her will, dividing her property equally between her daughters. In November, probably on the night of the twenty-second, as she took a candle to light a guest across the garden, her dress caught fire; and on November 24th *The Times* announced: "*Died:* Yesterday morning early, at

Wentworth-place, Hampstead, Mrs. Brawne, widow of the
late Samuel Brawne, Esq."

Perhaps Valentine made the funeral arrangements with
Stevenson, the undertaker in the High Street. Though there is
no record of an inquest or post-mortem, Mrs. Brawne was not
buried for nine days. The funeral took place on December 1st
at St. Martin-in-the-Fields, and her age was given as fifty-
seven. It is said that she was buried in Camden Town, in
St. Martin's burial ground, but her tomb cannot be seen there.
The cemetery has long been a public garden, bright with
dahlias in their season, where local children play throughout
the year.

Christmas marked the eleventh anniversary of Fanny's
betrothal, and the eighth on which the common rejoicing had
contrasted with her black dress. Four days later, on the morning
of December 29th, she received a letter from Brown. At a time
of extreme distress, it stirred her deepest feelings, and, like her
reply, it remains of primary importance in a study of her life.

Florence, 17 December 1829.

My dear Miss Brawne,
    Without any apology for our long silence, let me hope you are in
the best health, that your mother is better, and that Margaret is never
ailing; to which I add a merry Xmas and a happy new year to
all. Now, with these good wishes, I may begin.
    A few days ago, I received a letter from the Galignani in Paris
telling me they are on the eve of publishing the works of Keats, and
asking for his autograph. I sent it to them, with a letter stating it was
always my intention to write his life, and annex it to a Tragedy of his,
together with some unpublished poems in my possession, whenever
his countrymen should have learnt to value his poetry. I also told
them I believed that time was arrived, as needs it must, sooner or
later; but that I was fearful it was too late for me to enter into any
arrangement with them. Whatever their answer may be, I am
resolved to write his life, persuaded that no one, except yourself,

knew him better. Leigh Hunt's account of him is worse than disappointing; I cannot bear it; it seems as if Hunt was so impressed
by his illness, that he had utterly forgotten him in health. This is a
dreadful mistake, because it is our duty to his memory to show the
ruin his enemies had effected; and I will not spare them. It is not my
present purpose to enter into any criticism on his works, but to let
it be simply a biography; and, to make that as vivid as possible, I
shall incorporate into it passages from letters to me, and to his
brothers,—which last are in my possession; together with passages
from particular poems, or entire ones, relating to himself, always
avoiding those which regard you, unless you let me know that I may,
without mentioning your name, introduce them. There are, however,
two of his letters which I wish to give entire; one written when he
dispaired of Tom's recovery, the other when he dispaired of his own.
This latter one is of the most painful description; therefore I wish it to
be known, that Gifford and Lockhart may be thoroughly hated and
despised. The question is whether you will object to it; I think you
will not. Though much of it regards you, your name is never once
mentioned. Then again, those poems addressed to you, which you
permitted me to copy,—may I publish them? It is impossible for
me to judge of your feelings on the subject; but whatever they are,
you are certain that I shall obey them. To my mind, you ought to
consent, as no greater honour can be paid to a woman than to be
beloved by such a man as Keats. I am aware that, at a more recent
period, you would have been startled at its being alluded to; but
consider that eight years have now passed away; and now, no one,
if you do not, can object to it. Besides, Hunt has alluded to you
and what more will it be to give the poems addressed to that lady?
Your name will still remain as secret to the world as before. I shall
of course scrupulously avoid intimating who you are, or in what
part of England you reside. As his love for you formed so great a
part of him, we may be doing him an injustice in being silent on it:
Indeed something must be said especially as Hunt has said something.
We live among strange customs; for had you been husband and wife,
though but for an hour, every one would have thought himself at
liberty publicly to speak of, and all about you; but as you were so
only in your hearts, it seems, as it were, improper. Think of it in
your best train for thinking, my dear Miss Brawne, and let me know
your decision. I have turned it in my mind a great deal, and find
nothing,—to confess the truth freely,—against it.

9

Three months ago I heard you were at Bruges, on a visit to your aunt; but I suppose you are, by this time, returned. Give my kindest remembrances to Mrs. Brawne and Margaret. . . .

Believe me always

Your's most sincerely,

Chas. Brown.

Fanny sat down to answer his letter that morning. The corrections and false beginnings, the underlined phrases, misspellings and lack of punctuation in her draft reply suggest the immediate and profound disturbance of her mind. One sentence, removed from its context and published by Dilke's grandson in 1875, was to rouse the indignation of half-informed critics for more than sixty years.

Hampstead Decr 29th 1829

My dear Mr. Brown

As the aggressor I am too happy to escape the apologies I owe you on my long silence not gladly to take your hint and say nothing about it, the best reparation I can make is to answer your letter of today as soon as possible although I received it only this morning in the hours that have intervened before I sit down to answer it my feelings have entirely changed on the subject of the request it contains. Perhaps you will think I was opposed to it and am now come over to your side the question, but it [is] just just the contrary had I answered your letter immediately I should have told you that I considered myself so entirely unconnected with Mr Keats except by my own feelings that nothing published respecting him could affect me, but I now see it differently. We have all our little world in which we figure and I cannot help expressing some disinclination at the idea that the few acquaintance I have should be able to obtain such a key to my sensations. Having said so much you will probably conclude that I mean to refuse your request. Perhaps when I assure you that though my opinion has changed my intention of complying in every respect with your wishes remains, you will think I am mentioning my objections to make a favor of my consent but indeed my dear Mr Brown if you do, you mistake me entirely. It is only to justify myself I own that I state all I think. to you I am very grateful nor ought I to have gone so far without thanking you for your kindness and consideration in writing to me on the subject—I assure you I should not have hinted that your wishes were painful to me did I not feel the suffering myself to be even alluded to was a want of pride. So far am I from possessing overstrained delicacy that the circumstance of its being a mere love story is the least of my concern, on the contrary had I been his wife I should have felt my present reluctance would have been so much stronger that I think I must have made it my request that you would relinquish your intention. The only thing that saves me now is that so very few can know I am in any way implicated and that of those few I may hope the greater number may never see the book in Question. Do then entirely as you please and be assured that I comply with your wishes rather because they are yours than with the expectation of any good that can be done. I fear the kindest act would be to let him rest for ever in the obscurity to which unhappy circumstances have condemned him. Will the writings that remain of his rescue him from it? You can tell better than I, and are more impartial on the subject for my wish has long been that his name, his very name should be forgotten by every one but myself, that I have often wished most intensely.[20] *To your publishing his poems addressed to me I do not see there can be any objection* after the subject has been once alluded to, if you think them worthy of him. I entirely agree with you that if his life is to be published no part ought to be kept back for all you can show is his character, his life was too short and too unfortunate for any thing else. I have no doubt that his talents would have been great, not the less for their being developed rather late which I believe was the case, all I fear is whether he has left enough to make people believe that. If I could think so I should consider it right to make that sacrifice to his reputation that I now do to your kind motives. Not that even the establishment of his fame would give me the pleasure it ought. Without claiming too much constancy for myself I may truly say that he is well-remembered by me and that satisfied with that I could wish no one but myself knew he had ever existed but I confess as he was so much calumniated and suffered so much from it, it is perhaps the duty of those who loved and valued him to vindicate him also, and if it can be done, all the friends that time has left him and I above all must be deeply indebted to you. I am glad you feel that Mr Hunt gives him a weakness of character that only belonged to his ill health. Mr Hazlitt, if I remember rightly some remarks used five or six years ago is still more positive in fixing it on him. I should be glad if you

could disprove I was a very poor judge of character ten years ago
and probably overrated every good quality he had but surely they
go too far on the other side, after all he was but four and twenty when
his illness begun and he had gone through a great deal of vexation
before. . . .

Whether the fair and finished copy of this draft is in existence remains unknown; the original shows a mind distraught
by recent bereavement and by a long and even deeper grief.
But in this letter, written some nine years after Keats had died,
and at a time when only the first small sign of his immortality
could be discerned, Fanny Brawne showed an unselfish devotion to his fame and a width of understanding which her
contemporaries and many later lovers of Keats failed to comprehend. She who had loved him more deeply than his family
or friends, now claimed the supreme interest in his rightful
reputation; perhaps she decided even now that his letters to
her should one day be given to the public. And Monckton
Milnes, who suppressed her name, wrote with truth in 1848
that she had preserved the memory of Keats "with a sacred
honour."

Hampstead remained in 1830 a most delightful village, still
somewhat romantic yet pleasant in every way. Constable was
living in Well Walk, while Joanna Baillie, who had written
a play produced by Mrs. Siddons, lived on Windmill Hill,
and, as "a little old lady in a brown cloak and brown bonnet,"
used to pat small local children on the head. "She called me a
good little girl," recorded Rosa Rodd, "though I knew I was
nothing of the sort." Leigh Hunt would often walk over from
Highgate, and Fanny Brawne, in mourning as she had been
for nearly a decade, could be seen at Eliza Taylor's in Church
Row, buying toys for the two-year-old niece of Keats. By March
the Brawnes' house was empty; Margaret may have gone to live
with relations, perhaps the Richardsons in St. Marylebone. It

is thought that Fanny moved next door,[21] to remain with Keats's sister, who remembered the agreement made in Pancras Lane, long ago.

On May Day she took Irene to watch the chimney-sweeps' carnival: Jack-in-the-Green, inside an ivy-covered cage, spun round while the clown and a piper danced about him, and the May Queen, who carried a shining brass ladle, collected money from the spectators. At Whitsun they saw the village sports on the White Bear Green, when boys would climb a greasy pole for the tempting leg of mutton on top. In the summer there were cricket matches on Shepherd's Green, and itinerant musicians, playing the clarinet, flute, 'cello and double bass, and singing in harmony, wandered through the streets. This year the Metropolitan Police were first seen in Hampstead; and in November, the vestry sent a deputation to Sir Robert Peel to ask that the new and costly guardians might be withdrawn. The deputation was received by an undersecretary, and soon afterwards Hampstead resigned itself to the expense.

It was nowadays "a large and respectable populous village and parish"; within Fanny's lifetime it had doubled in size. In 1831 it had well over eight thousand inhabitants, twenty-seven taverns and public houses and twenty-nine academies and schools; and the list of gentry in this, her last year at Wentworth Place, reads like a valediction to her circle of acquaintances and friends. Burridge Davenport, who had "no light and shade," who had befriended Keats and entertained Fanny herself, moved to Bloomsbury before the end of the decade; Charles Elley became chief clerk in the bankruptcy office, and commissioner for taking affidavits in the palatine court of Lancaster; and Dr. Lord, the poor medical officer and the Brawnes' friend and physician, who described the vestry as "dumb dogs who could not bite," became none the less the first medical officer of health for Hampstead. He held the post for twenty-two

years and suggested many reforms, among them baths and
wash-houses for the poor, and he lived long enough to know
that these were at last provided by the parish. Another figure
became, in time,[22] familiar in the village: James Hessey,
Taylor's partner, left publishing and took "a large old school
at Hampstead," Johnson's School at Norway House, and
among his pupils was Arthur Elley Finch. It is pleasant to
think of a cousin of Fanny Brawne learning *The Eve of St.
Agnes* from Keats's publisher: one could choose no better final
glimpse of the family in Hampstead.

In September, at Wentworth Place, Fanny Llanos's third
child was born, and named Juan after his uncle who had once
lived there; and in November Fanny Brawne's aunt, Elizabeth
Baker, died. The Llanos were too numerous now to live in the
small house, and by March 1832 they had gone; their destina-
tion remains unknown. It seems, however, that the Bakers left
Kent and settled abroad, and within a year both the Brawnes
were living with them.

"The Brawnes," wrote Dilke to George Keats in February
1833, "are still single & residing with an uncle and cousins in
France": though records have been destroyed, it is known that
they spent some time in Boulogne. Built on the summit and
slopes of the hills skirting the Liane, the town seemed designed
to please all lovers of the picturesque. The small Haute Ville
on top of the hill was encircled by medieval ramparts and
entered by ancient gateways, a thirteenth-century château
graced the town; and on the high ground above Boulogne, and
as yet incomplete, stood the Colonne de la Grande Armée,
celebrating Napoleon's projected invasion of England. Here,
where he made his preparations, the great Doric pillar rose
nearly two hundred feet high, to be surmounted by his imperial
likeness. From the foot of the town to the busy harbour lay the
Basse Ville, for Boulogne was not only an historic town but a
flourishing centre of commerce.

It was an obvious home for merchants like the Lindos; and in Boulogne, according to her granddaughter,[23] Fanny Brawne met Louis Lindo, her future husband.

## VII

♦♦♦

THE LINDOS were one of the oldest and most respected Sephardic Jewish families. Louis Lindo's great-grandfather, Abraham, who lived to be nearly a hundred, was recorded by Lysons in *The Environs of London*; Louis's grandfather, Alexander, was engaged at the beginning of the century in the West Indian trade, and his house was renowned for wealth and integrity, sending "immense shipments" to the French West Indies: the draft for £260,000 received from Napoleon was, however, dishonoured on a frivolous pretext, and this injustice had brought Lindo to the verge of ruin. He had been one of the few remaining merchant princes among the Portuguese Jews. His son, David Alexander, the father of Louis Lindo, became an underwriter at Lloyds, and in 1805 he married Matilda Prager Salomons. In 1808 they moved to Bloomsbury Square, where they lived (for a time a few doors from the Disraelis) during the next twelve years. Their children were born in fairly rapid succession: Alexander in 1808, Mary Anne in 1809, Harriet the following year, and Louis on May 12th, 1812; Mary or Maria followed in 1814, Mark Prager in 1819 and Philip Moravier in 1821.

By this time the family had moved to Burton Crescent; in 1825, David Alexander Lindo, described as a merchant, took a house in Percy Street, and here the family apparently remained until the end of 1827. They later settled in Boulogne, where they lived until April 1832.

Most of them were eventually converted to the Church of England, but they seem to have embraced widely different interests with their natural Jewish vitality: Alexander, who remained a member of the synagogue, became a London solicitor; Mark suffered the discipline of an English boarding school at Boulogne and later described his experiences in a novel: indeed he seems to have turned all misfortunes to good account, for, locked in his father's library as a punishment for misdeeds, he acquired the beginnings of the knowledge that earned him a name as novelist and translator, the title of Inspector of Primary Education in The Hague, and, eventually, a university chair. Philip began his career as an artist, continued it as a deputy director of gasworks in The Hague, and made his reputation by inventing a safety coupling for railway carriages and exploring the possibilities of cement.

Mark and Philip were schoolboys when Fanny first met them. Louis Lindo could not have been more than twenty. He wanted to travel and to enjoy his youth before he accepted some dull commercial routine; he had strong interest and per-haps ability in the arts, and he showed not only those merits of his own which must have been exceptional, but a little of that ardent character which she had ever loved. He offered her, in her thirties, the youthfulness which had vanished so long from her life, and it seemed a return to her early days at Elm Cottage and Wentworth Place, when she had known the warm affec-tion of her family, the companionship and eager love of the gifted and the young.

She agreed to marry Louis Lindo as soon as he should come of age; it would then be more than twelve years since Keats had died. And it is some measure of Fanny's strength of character that until seven or eight years after her marriage her husband was to know nothing of Keats's love. "He never would have heard of it," she wrote to Mrs. Dilke, "had it not happened ... he noticed the portrait in your room; and asked who it was. As you hesitated in answering, he felt puzzled & I, to prevent awkward mistakes in future, when we got home explained as much as was necessary." He still had "a very imperfect idea of the real case."

On May 12th, 1833, Louis Lindo came of age, and by June he was living in St. Marylebone. Fanny was staying at 3, Middlesex Place with Ann Richardson, one perhaps of the three Miss Richardsons who had obstinately copied Margaret's clothes. On Saturday, June 15th, she married him by licence at St. Marylebone Parish Church. Four witnesses signed the register: Alexander, the bridegroom's brother, John Gould of Hampton, M. L. Dunnage, perhaps from Walthamstow, and Ann Richardson.

Fanny Llanos was not present, for the marriage "she neither understood nor excused."[24] As a very old lady she took continual interest in Fanny's children, but perhaps she felt that the intended wife of Keats should have remained for ever his widowing love. Her judgment, if such it was, seems ungenerous and blind, for Fanny Brawne, who had loved Keats with devotion through all her youth, would love the remembrance of him to the end of her life; but she was too vigorous to remain content with a memory. And those who had watched her long "widowhood" with sympathy could have found only satisfaction in the announcement in Monday's *Times*.

Five months later a more spectacular marriage was solemnized in France. The Chevalier da Cunha had been successively Comptroller to the Empress Dona Leopoldina of Habsburg, Secretary to the Embassy Extraordinary to the Court of Lisbon, and chargé d'affaires in London, Paris and Berlin; and in 1833, a lieutenant-colonel in the Brazilian service, he had a distinguished career ahead of him. He was living in the Rue de la Barre, Dieppe, the same street as the Baker family and Margaret Brawne. How long he had known her must remain a matter for speculation, but his social eminence was matched by her

remarkable beauty; on November 30th they were married
by the Mayor of Dieppe and by the minister of the English
Church.

As Fanny and her husband were not present at Margaret's
wedding, it seems that they may already have joined the Lindo
family who for nearly two years had been living in Pempelfort,
a suburb of Duesseldorf. Years later, in his novel *Le Saltim-
banque*, Mark Lindo described the social life of Duesseldorf,
thinly disguising the city as Pumpenheim; and one can imagine
Fanny listening to the grenadiers' weekly concert in the park,
drinking a little *kirsch* in her coffee, and watching the beau-
monde: the officers stride with a clatter of swords down the
gravelled paths, the court marshal, accompanied by his portly
wife and daughters, sits placidly at his table, lighting a cigar,
and innumerable minor functionaries and tall thin subalterns
play dice and quiz the passers-by.

Sometimes the Lindos would go by river to Cologne: its
medieval towers rose from the Rhine, its ancient walls had
not yet been destroyed. They explored the dark tortuous alleys
of the old inner town, and the Gothic cathedral in which lay
buried the heart of Marie de Medici; they marvelled at the
shrine, adorned with gold and jewels, which took its name
from the three Kings of Cologne, the three wise men, it was
said, who had adored the infant Christ. And as the summer
approached, Fanny enjoyed these travels with a new tranquillity: she was expecting her first child.

On Saturday, July 26th, which would have been the thirtieth
birthday of Samuel, her brother, Fanny's son was born. He was
called Vernon after his maternal grandfather and that now
distant ancestor who had acted at Drury Lane. He took his
first name, Edmund, perhaps from Kean or Spenser, both of
whom his mother had admired. "If you should have a Boy do
not christen him John . . . 'Tis a bad name, and goes against a
Man. If my name had been Edmund I should have been more

fortunate." It was the name which Keats himself would have chosen.

Fanny's movements during the next two years are difficult to trace. After her marriage, wrote her granddaughter, "owing to delicate health, she mostly lived in Germany, with occasional visits to Boulogne and to London." After the birth of Edmund, Louis Lindo became an officer in the British Legion in Spain, and distinguished himself for courage fighting the Carlists. Fanny seems to have stayed in England with her child. At last, however, receiving no news from her husband, she wrote to his colonel: Louis had been seriously ill and was suffering from loss of memory. Fanny, taking Edmund with her, went out to Spain at once and brought her husband home.

But a southern climate suited her best, and by the spring of 1838 she was once more on the Continent. She and her husband were living in the Maison Etcheverry, in the Mousse-rolles quarter of Bayonne, and here, at ten o'clock on the night of May 22nd, her second child, also a boy, was born. The birth was registered by "Sieur Louis Lindo, âgé de 32 ans, rentier," who was in fact just twenty-six. He declared the child's name to be Herbert, and Fanny added that of Valentine. It was, as she had said, "a pretty name," and, born within a few miles of the frontier, her son might prove "everything that a Spanish cavalier ought to be."

In the late thirties and early forties the Lindos must have enjoyed some experience of Vienna, where the Chevalier da Cunha was Brazilian Minister. "The poor, idiotic, big-headed Ferdinand and his lovely, saintly, Italian empress"[25] led a court of extraordinary brilliance. Each ambassador had the privilege of keeping two *coureurs* to run beside his carriage on state occasions, and the da Cunhas entertained Princess Esterhazy, Prince Metternich, whose charm had become a legend, the Princess Lichtenstein, who looked like the goddess Juno, and the mature but magnificent Stephanie of Bedan, daughter of Josephine de Beauharnais. Yet Margaret da Cunha was so remarkable for her beauty that the Emperor called her the handsomest woman at court.[26]

Vienna was the capital of Germanic gaiety: "Thousands and tens of thousands were seated in the gardens, netting, knitting, listening to the bands, drinking coffee and sugar-water, and eating ices. There was the Folk's Theatre, with its comic representations; the opera; there were concerts, and fireworks all in full action. Imperial gardens and parks were open, and the public walked in them and through the very courts and gateways of palaces, as if they were their own"; archdukes and princes sat in public places, drinking coffee with their friends, and the Emperor himself would walk among his subjects as if he were a common citizen. Fanny commemorated in her scrapbook the crimson and gold interiors of the theatres and the austere splendour of St. Stephen's Cathedral. Steamers had just begun to take passengers down the Danube to Budapest,[27] and she delighted in the coronet of towers, uneven roofs and palaces as it rose, gradually, from the river; she recorded the white Cziráky palace, the pink carriage waiting at the gates, the sunlit coaches bowling down the Wienergasse, the shuttered Marzibanische palace in the Göttergasse, the footmen in scarlet livery, the officers wearing plumed caps and crimson and blue; and she and Louis went on to Prague, where at evening the turrets and steeples, the fluted tiles on the roofs, glowed in the setting sun, and the distant hills loomed purple across the river.

Early in the 1840's they went to live in Heidelberg. The old university town attracted more than one figure on the periphery of literature. Among the students, devotees of duelling, tobacco and beer, leading a hermit's life, was the grandson of Goethe; Mary Howitt dashed through the streets on a handsome horse-drawn sledge to play Blind Man's Buff and drink coffee at

Neckargemünd; and an ex-lieutenant of dragoons with the nominal rank of captain, Shelley's first cousin, "a man of culture and intelligence," was showing every attention to the English colony. Thomas Medwin, who provided the Howitts with English newspapers, and had published such books as the *Conversations of Lord Byron,* had for years collected and invented biographical details about Byron and Shelley. He was always, as Fanny expressed it, "on the hunt for literary prey," and the Lindos had not been long in Heidelberg before he "stumbled on the Shakespeare with Mr. Keats name written in it."

Fanny judged Medwin's unscholarly and unscrupulous nature well enough to hide some of her other treasures. "If Medwin had known that I possessed the Cenci by Shelly marked with many of Keats notes he would have been miserable till he got it, but I kept that and others out of his way." He asked her occasional questions, but they had no detailed discussion until Mrs. Shelley's *Essays, Letters from Abroad* fell into her hands. Mrs. Shelley had quoted a letter from Robert Finch, Severn's friend, which professed to describe Keats on his deathbed.

By this "very unnecessary" publication Fanny was "much shocked . . . it gave an account of the last few weeks of poor Keats life that I wondered Mr Severn did not contradict." She showed to Medwin Severn's letter to her mother "which gave such a different picture," and he asked her to let him publish it. Fanny's sense of delicacy prevented her from disclosing more: "I must tell you, I in no way brought *myself* in, to Captain Medn., but spoke of that letter and another as having been addressed to my mother, which they were"; but she allowed him also, in his coming *Life of Shelley,* to use Keats's letter written from Naples Harbour. She showed him the Spenser and let him take a copy of the miniature. And to his biography she contributed her own account of Keats's character: it shows that in middle age she retained that loving and tolerant understanding which Keats himself, and Brown, had long since recognized.

When, in 1847, the book appeared, Severn wrote Medwin a strong letter: the publication of part of his correspondence was, in his view, illegal. "I was not aware that any *legal* objection existed," Fanny told Mrs. Dilke. "There could be no other as it only does Mr. Severn credit & he has been anxious himself to bring it forward. As this is the case, & he must have guessed from whom the extract from his letter was obtained, I think that which he wrote to Capt. Medwin quite uncalled for. At the same time, I should be sorry for any ill feeling to exist between myself & Mr. Severn, whose kindness I have always appreciated.—so if you have an opportunity, you may just say, I am sorry I did not know of his *legal* rights."

It seems that before the *Life of Shelley* appeared Medwin had been gossiping with his friend Mrs. de Crespigny.* She had a bent for literature, already knew the Lindos (or Lindons, as they had come to be called); she could hardly remain content with half the truth. She "asked Mr. Lindon, on his next visit, whether Mr. Keats had been an admirer of Mrs. Lindon's— and he, taken by surprise, knew just enough to answer yes."

In 1840, in Smith's standard library, and exactly copied from the Galignani edition, there appeared the first reprint in England of the collected poems of Keats: it marked the quiet beginning of public interest. In the spring of 1841 George Keats agreed to the publication of a memoir and literary remains, and Charles Brown, about to emigrate to New Zealand, sent his Keatsiana to that farsighted biographer, Richard Monckton Milnes: the parcel was the basis of the *Life, Letters and Literary Remains* which were published seven years later. Brown's memoir was read by Dilke and Severn, and Dilke considered it unfit for publication: it contained much, he wrote, "which could not, without profanation, be breathed into the cold ear of an indifferent public—to say nothing of certain references to Mrs. L. which could not but be deeply painful to her." Fanny was in England in 1841 and Severn asked to see her; it was twenty years since Keats's death and she could not receive him "for deep emotion."

In the delicate allusions of Hunt, the diplomatic references of Brown, she had already entered literary history. The year 1843 brought the publication of *The Life of Gerald Griffin* and his reminiscences of the Brawnes at Wentworth Place, and within a few months, in *Imagination and Fancy*, Hunt instinctively touched the heart of *St. Agnes' Eve*: Keats, he declared, is "as much in love with his heroine as his hero is . . . he, doubtless, wrote as he felt, for he was also deeply in love; and extreme sensibility struggled in him with a great understanding." Fanny probably read *Imagination and Fancy*; she had long ago subscribed to Hunt's *Poetical Works*; through all her travels she had carried with her his *Literary Pocket Book* and Keats's copy of *Foliage*, and she continued, almost certainly, to read his poetry and criticism both for remembrance' sake and from her love of literature. Middleaged, she might see again in *The Eve of St. Agnes* the exquisite reflection of her youth.

The day after her fortyfourth birthday she gave birth to her only daughter. The child was called Margaret, after Madame da Cunha, Emily, a popular Victorian name, and Walworth, to remind her perhaps of her greatgrandfather, who had established the fortunes of the Ricketts family and had lived in the village of Walworth nearly four decades ago.

Monckton Milnes, with the willing assistance of the Keats circle, was at last preparing the *Life, Letters and Literary Remains*. It was time to explode the myth that Keats had been killed by critics, and late in 1845 Severn wrote, candidly, asking Milnes to publish "the real cause of [Keats's] death. . . . I mean the poor fellows anguish at the first symptoms of consumption

when he was about to be married to a most lovely & accom/
plished girl, which anguish never ceasd. . . . This Lady was a
Miss Brawn, she was possessed of considerable property in
addition to her beauty & youth & was devotedly attached to
Keats & his fame. . . . Now do take this as the serious wind
up of his life—the critique make mention of in its place but only
as the poor fellows least misfortune."

In 1847 there appeared Medwin's *Life of Shelley* with Fanny's
anonymous but significant statement, and the same year Howitt
described the farewell of Keats and "the young lady to whom he
was engaged." To the public the fact of Keats's love had long
been revealed, and to his biographer the identity of Fanny
Brawne was known: indeed, it seems that Milnes corresponded
with Fanny, for he quoted a stanza written by Keats in her
copy of Spenser, and perhaps it was she who confirmed her
devotion to Keats, only asking that her name should be with/
held. However, Milnes, misplacing one of Keats's letters,
identified Fanny Brawne with Charmian, and to this half/
imaginary love he referred with Victorian diplomacy, for
"where . . . the persons in question . . . may be still alive, it will
at once be felt how indecorous would be any conjectural analy/
sis of such sentiments. . . . It is enough that [the object of his
love] has preserved his memory with a sacred honour, and it is
no vain assumption, that to have inspired and sustained the
one passion of this noble being has been a source of grave
delight and earnest thankfulness, through the changes and
chances of her earthly pilgrimage."

When the book appeared in 1848, Fanny received a copy
from the publisher; she may have been in Frankfort at the time,
for she kept an engraving of the city and dated it. Her travels
remain a series of speculations: according to her scrapbook, she
went to Ratisbon, where the huge painting in the  Goliath/
strasse caught her attention, and on to Weinheim and Staltzen/
fels and the many castles which frowned across the Rhine. She

and her husband may have visited relations: Mark Lindo, settled in Arnhem, or Philip, painting in Duesseldorf. In 1853 the name of Louis Lindon first appeared in a Freiburg almanack.

His occupation in Freiburg is difficult to determine: perhaps he was still a *rentier*, or gentleman of independent means, perhaps he taught languages; it may be that in this fertile duchy, known for its wines, he began his work in a firm of wine-growers. His parents had died within two years of one another, and the Lindons' link with Duesseldorf grew weaker; Fanny sold some of her property in England, and in Freiburg the family settled for several years, only moving from the Kartaeu-serstrasse to the Bahnhofstrasse, from house to house. It was during one of these removals that Fanny was told to keep her eyes on the Lindon plate chest; so absorbed was she in her book that all instructions were forgotten. The family silver was taken away and never seen again.[28]

She was in her fifties now, but she looked remarkably young.[29] She had changed very little: many years abroad had not assuaged her interest in travel. She still found it at times "a great exertion" to write letters, but she remained an insatiable reader: she scrutinized newspapers, delighted in fashion journals, and pursued her favourite subjects, however out-of-the-way, with perseverance. She could answer any question on historical costume at a moment's notice; in her scrapbook the prints of Regency dresses and Byronic turbans had only been succeeded by those of Victorian tartan skirts and four-tier crinolines. She had lost none of her candour, and as she had once discussed Cobbett and the Westminster electors, so she had come to argue warmly about Palmerston. It was now more than thirty years since Keats had died, but of him she would rarely speak; her letters from him she never mentioned, except to tell her children to guard them carefully. One day, she knew, they would be given to the public, and if the biography of Keats should be written, "nothing ought to be kept back."

The fame of Keats was increasing, her own legend growing stronger; and as Monckton Milnes himself still confused her with Charmian, his followers can hardly be blamed for their misunderstanding: "It was Keats's body," Lowell wrote in 1854, "that needed to have its equilibrium restored, the waste of his nervous energy that must be repaired by deep draughts of the overflowing life and drowsy tropical force of an abundant and healthily-poised womanhood. . . . This glimpse of her, with her leopardess beauty, crossing the room and drawing men after her magnetically, is all we have. She seems to have been still living in 1848, and as Mr. Milnes tells us, kept the memory of the poet sacred. 'She is an East Indian,' Keats says, 'and ought to be her grandfather's heir.' Her name we do not know."

At last, in 1859, when their younger son had finished his education in Germany, the Lindons returned to England. They settled in London, perhaps already at 34, Coleshill Street, a pleasant, unpretentious house, one of a row in Pimlico; by some coincidence it was a few doors from the house where Severn had led "a dressing-gowny artistic existence." They may have been neighbours for a time, but at the end of 1860 Severn returned to Rome as British Consul.

It is said[30] that Edmund Lindon, inheriting his parents' love of travel, went to remote parts of the world; Herbert entered the Store Office at Woolwich and later worked at the War Office, while by 1861 Louis Lindon had become a mining agent in Broad Street Buildings. There is only one mention of his agency, and it seems very probable that Sir Charles Dilke, a Commissioner, enlisted his services for the second Exhibition.[31] Speaking French, and German, possibly Spanish and Dutch, Louis Lindon would have proved himself an able secretary, but the appointment must have been either junior or informal, as it is unrecorded. In his later years he was agent to the firm of Ruinart, champagne growers of Rheims, and worked (as the younger John Ricketts had done) in St. Swithin's Lane.[32]

The only members of the Keats circle whom Fanny still knew were Dilke, who was now past seventy, and his only son; Mrs. Dilke had long since died. All the ambitions of his devoted parents Charley had amply fulfilled, and he had declined a knighthood for his services in 1851 only to receive a baronetcy now. Occasionally Fanny and her husband would go down to Alice Holt, the house in Hampshire to which Dilke himself had retired. He still grew vegetables with the anxious care he had shown at Wentworth Place, and "hands in Pockets making observations," he escorted Fanny round his garden. He spoke proudly of his grandson at Cambridge and discussed his own literary research, and perhaps, to him, Fanny would talk of Keats.

It was towards the end of her life, and oppressed by grave financial troubles, that she made a decision which hurt her deeply. Rather than expose it to the indignity of public auction she sold, to Dilke, Severn's miniature of Keats. It was a perfect likeness of him in the winter of their betrothal nearly half a century ago, and she had first possessed it, "beautifully set," a little before his death. For her, who still wore his ring and a lock of his hair, who treasured his books and carried his letters with her always, who even now could not speak of him without emotion, the decision was a hard one; but to Dilke she wrote at last: "I am induced to ask whether it would suit you to purchase that miniature of Mr. Keats which has been for so long a time in my possession. It would not be a light motive that would make me part with it, but I have this satisfaction, that next to my own family, there is no one in whose possession I should . . ." The fragmentary letter breaks off, and continues: "I would ask you to at once remit the money to Mr. Lindon, but as he knows nothing of the transaction, I enclose a note which will explain it to him, if you will send it at the same time." It was indeed no casual transaction, no mercenary trading on the past: to her husband's future she could have made no greater sacrifice.

In these, the last years of her life, the star of her poet was rising: "What a poet," Landor had written, "would poor Keats have been, had he lived! He had something of Shakespeare in him, and (what nobody else ever had) much, very much of Chaucer." Tennyson already set him above "Wordsworth, Coleridge, Byron, Shelley, every one of them . . . if he had lived he would have been the greatest of us all"; Coventry Patmore said that "if Keats had lived ten years longer he would have been the greatest man we ever had." Barry Cornwall, who had met Keats, recognized that "if, like Lucifer, he has not drawn after him a third part of the heavens, he has had a radiant train of followers . . . all who have since succeeded in distinguishing themselves in the same sphere of art." "He was," Rossetti recorded later, "among all his contemporaries who established their names, the one true heir of Shakespeare."

The circle of those who had known him was finally disintegrating: George had been dead for more than twenty years, Fanny Llanos had been lost to sight; Haydon, his imaginary genius unrecognized, had taken his own life, and Reynolds was only remembered by the inscription on his tombstone: "The Friend of Keats." Hunt had gone, paying homage to Keats until the very last; Brown had died long ago in New Zealand, and his grave would be forgotten; Severn remained in Rome, reliving the past; and the year 1864 brought the death of Taylor, and of Charles Wentworth Dilke who in building Wentworth Place had changed the course of literature.

Fanny herself was sixty-five and inclined to be frail. The Brawnes had never been physically strong, and Fanny's father, both her brothers and one of her sisters had died prematurely.

She herself had long been asthmatic and had lived abroad for most of her married life to escape the northern climate. As the winter of 1865 drew near, she suffered from angina pectoris. Her asthma returned, the two complaints aggravated one another, and in the first days of December she felt the imminence of death.

And, her appreciation sharpened by dying as that of Keats had been, she, too, thought of green fields, and mused with the greatest affection on every flower and tree she had known from her infancy: buttercups in the fields at West End, wild anemones on the Heath, the hedge of laurustinus and china roses, the mulberry tree. Devoted wife and mother though she remained, loving her husband and children with unselfish affection, perhaps in her final moments she thought of Keats; and now in this drear Victorian December she remembered him, almost half a century ago, telling her at Elm Cottage, on Christmas Day, that he had found in her his poetic ideal: "The richness, the bloom, the full form, the enchantment of love after my own heart."

# Epilogue
## 1865-1937

FANNY BRAWNE, who had entered the world obscurely, left it almost unnoticed. Her death was only briefly recorded on December 8th, in *The Times*: "On the 4th inst., at 34, Coleshill Street, Eaton-square, FRANCES, the wife of LOUIS LINDON, Esq. Friends will kindly accept this intimation." She was buried next day in Brompton Cemetery. Some time later the family moved to 20, Gloucester Terrace, a small but pleasant house in Kensington, and here, on October 21st, 1872, in his sixty-first year, Louis Lindon died: he was buried in the same grave as his wife. A short announcement appeared in *The Times*, but it was left for *The Athenaeum* to make the pregnant and extraordinary statement: "We have to mention the death of Mr. Louis Lindon, an old friend of the Keats family."

In the same issue of *The Athenaeum*, by some curious chance, "An Admirer of Keats" asked what had become of Keats's Shakespeare. It had been inherited by Margaret Lindon, and in mid-November the correspondent wrote again: "Keats's Shakespeare is, by the great kindness of its owner, now in my hands. It belongs to the daughter of the lady to whom Keats gave it, and to whom he gave also his Spenser which cannot for the moment be found. The possessor of the Shakespeare has also some most interesting letters about Keats: for instance, one from his publishers (not Taylor & Hessey) lamenting the *badness* and unsaleableness of his works." Soon afterwards Sir Charles Dilke bought the Shakespeare from Herbert Lindon; it was probably one of several relics, including the Olliers' letter, which passed at the time into his possession, and he purchased the love-letters to prevent their publication.

"I remember," his private secretary writes of a later period, "seeing Sir Charles put some of Keats's letters in the fire, as he thought they were not things that should be seen by anyone."[1] In all probability he destroyed Keats's letter to Dilke written on board the *Maria Crowther*: it would have revealed much about Fanny Brawne. The Dilke letters, including those bought from Severn and the Lindons, had for years been "calculated by the bushel": they made an imposing burnt offering to the Victorian gods.

In 1875, however, Fanny Brawne was brought into the light: there appeared *The Papers of a Critic, selected from the writings of the late Charles Wentworth Dilke, with a biographical sketch by his grandson*. It is strange that Sir Charles Dilke, whose grandparents and father had known Keats and Fanny Brawne, and who himself loved the poet's work and memory, should have chosen to publish about Fanny just those comments which were unkind; for Mrs. Dilke's note and Jane Reynolds's remark on the "most unhappy connexion" he printed with one sentence which had been written by Fanny herself in a moment of anguish and which, cut from its context, would be readily misunderstood: "The kindest act would be to let him rest for ever in the obscurity to which unhappy circumstances have condemned him." Published some sixty years before her letters to Keats's sister, this quotation bred the legend of Fanny Brawne which has been long in dying.

To Monckton Milnes, now Lord Houghton, who was preparing a memoir for the Aldine edition of Keats, Sir Charles sent Jane Reynolds's acid note, commenting "I quite agree with it." Lord Houghton was shown the love-letters and apparently considered them unfit to be published in full, but when his memoir appeared in 1876 some of them were quoted. By the end of the year, Herbert Lindon had asked Sir Charles Dilke to return the letters to him; they were given back, with one exception, and on December 29th he offered them to

Lord Houghton. Fortunately for posterity the offer was refused;
and, acting according to his legal rights and in the deepest
interests of literature, Herbert Lindon showed them to
Mr. Harry Buxton Forman,[2] to whose broad vision and
scrupulous research all lovers of Keats are indebted. To the poet's
sister Mr. Forman wrote later: "These letters, to my mind, set
him right with posterity; and thus it came to be, to me, a sacred
duty to take all the risk of personal opprobrium that might
attach to counselling and abetting their publication."[3]

When they discussed with Mr. Forman the letters to appear
in print, the Lindons "fully considered what was proper for
publication"; they identified Keats's description of their
mother, which "answered to the facts in every particular except
that of age," and they told Mr. Forman of "one or two personal
traits." Fanny Llanos, who was now seventy-four, wrote to
him from Spain assuring him that Charmian "was not Miss
Brawne, she not being an East Indian nor having a Grandfather living at that time," and on the authority of Keats's
sister Lord Houghton's error was corrected. When Severn
heard of the existence of the letters, he was "astonished with
delight for they must be even superior to Keats's poetry & will
be a boon to the world quite unlooked for";[4] throughout the
autumn of 1877, letters passed between Severn in Scala Dante
and Mr. Forman in Marlborough Hill, discussing the site of
Elm Cottage, allusions to the Hampstead circle, the Bright
Star Sonnet, and the appearance of Wentworth Place, and,
aided by Mr. Forman's diagram, Severn tried to reconstruct
the house as he had known it some sixty years ago. "My
memory has been fairly taxed," he admitted to his sister,[5] "and
has just come up to the mark, the work is dedicated to me and
so 'twas my duty to aid all I could on this account, added to
which my regard for the memory of the Poet and my joy at
these 37 letters which I am told are of a beauty beyond his
poems. . . . I expect you'll see Keats new work in the papers for

Mr. Buxton Forman tells me there has never been anything like it."

In February 1878 the *Letters of John Keats to Fanny Brawne* were published. They were received with a "vulgar outcry of pressmen" on both sides of the Atlantic. A critic in *Scribner's Magazine*, reviewing the American edition, declared that Keats's "mistake was fatal with regard to this woman, and his approaching death a merciful release." *The Spectator* considered the publication "decidedly unbecoming. . . . You might almost as fitly reproduce the actual lovers' talks and sighs of the present day for our posterity fifty years hence, by the help of the talking phonograph. . . . Yet who," asked the writer, "would dream of making love in the presence of a talking phonograph?" That Keats had read Fanny Brawne's letters during service in a cathedral was actually believed, and raised the fire of Victorian churchgoers: "Rather a cynical peripatetic pleasure," one of them observed, "that can only have been taken not very considerately for the worship of others." The reviewer in *Notes and Queries* remarked that the publication could "only be excused, if excusable at all, by the pride of possession and by the eagerness of admiring curiosity"; while Sir Charles Dilke, who had come to own *The Athenaeum*, castigated in his journal Mr. Forman, the Lindons, and Fanny Brawne herself: if the publication, he wrote, "is the greatest impeachment of a woman's sense of womanly delicacy to be found in the history of literature, Mr. Forman's extraordinary preface is no less notable as a sign of the degradation to which the bookmaker has sunk . . . what are we to say if this hideous breach of the sanctities of life is done with the implied warrantry of the woman to whom the letters were addressed?—of her who should, indeed, have 'carefully guarded' them—not because 'they would some day be considered of value,' but because she could not part with such sacred things till her death approached—and then have burnt them or ordered them to be buried with her. Such a woman was Fanny Brawne, if we are to accept Mr. Forman's portrait of her; which, however, we refuse to do."

Fanny Llanos's first impression of the letters "was most painful," and Severn read them "with great pain," understanding *"for the first time* the suffering & death of the Poet"; to both of them Mr. Forman wrote, explaining the publication with all his eloquence and understanding. "May heaven reward you," Fanny Llanos answered, "for your affection towards the memory of my poor brother"; and Severn, who was old and ill, offered to help prepare the library edition of Keats.

A single critic felt that the letters stood unexplained until the other side of the correspondence was known. But the book had burst upon a public who were immature to receive it. One reader simply professed[6] that the letters added "nothing to our knowledge of the poet's character and life," and "surely," he wrote, "it is not well for those who love his poetry to see him thus; the painful impression . . . will be with them when they turn again to *Endymion,* or *Lamia,* or the sonnets." The childish unwillingness to recognize facts, the confusion of Victorian prudery with permanent literary values is to us incredible. It seemed that the legend of "poor Keats" must be retained and strengthened; and if he had not been killed by *The Quarterly,* he must, as Sir Charles Dilke had said, have been killed by his passion; and love was only fatal when it was unrequited.

That the value of the letters, which Fanny Brawne had mentioned, had been literary and not commercial, was a thought which did not occur to the Victorians. That disease had made Keats suspicious and morbidly possessive was an explanation not to be considered. In the light of their sentimental traditions about the poet, their ignorance of his love, the Victorians drew Fanny Brawne as they wanted her to be: a common, shallow, faithless, calculating flirt. Until her letters to Fanny Keats appeared in 1937, the portrait was generally accepted.

Throughout the 1880's the Victorian attitude to Fanny Brawne remained unchanged and her letters from Keats continued to shock and unsettle the critics. Matthew Arnold, who set Keats with Shakespeare, was inclined to speak "even as *Blackwood* or the *Quarterly* were in the old days wont to speak; one is tempted to say that Keats's love-letter is the love-letter of a surgeon's apprentice. It has in its relaxed self-abandonment something underbred and ignoble, as of a youth ill brought up." Social standing, like financial status, was almost a tenet of Victorian literary criticism. John Gilmer Speed, the great-nephew of the poet, in a memoir in 1883, took it "for granted that no one who will care to read this book will care to be told anything more about Keats's love for Fanny Brawne than he himself tells in the painful and pathetic letters herein published." Rossetti, whose *Life of John Keats* appeared in 1887, considered it a pity that Fanny Brawne "was wont, after Keats's death, to speak of him . . . as 'that foolish young poet who was in love with me'"; the authenticity of the remark is not now worth discussion, but the Victorians accepted it. The same year saw the publication of Colvin's *Life of Keats* in the series "English Men of Letters." He wrote with sympathy and reprinted Fanny's statement to Medwin, a "truer and kinder appreciation of the poet . . . than might be gathered from her phrase in the letter . . . so often quoted"; yet even he could not mention the love-letters without observing that "their publication must be regretted by all who hold that human respect and delicacy are due to the dead no less than to the living, and to genius no less than to obscurity."

One Victorian scholar there was, however, who saw beyond the age: Mr. Forman, preparing to edit all the known writings of Keats. He called on Sir Charles Dilke in the house in Sloane

Street to which so much Keatsiana had found its way. "When I approached him," Mr. Forman remembered,[7] "we were mutually aware of a divergence of view on the question of the Fanny Brawne letters, and particularly on the personality of the poet's *innamorata*. Nevertheless, when I had laid before him the details of my project and method, he decided . . . to support the undertaking by giving me unrestrained access to all his material. . . . From this friendly and helpful attitude he never swerved." There had followed a remarkable interview in which the Dilke collection, the gifts from Keats himself to the family, the former possessions of Fanny Brawne, the purchases from Severn and his children, were spread out and sorted. Gradually there rose from the carpet a pile more bulky than Mr. Forman could carry; and he left in a cab with Keats's Milton and the folio Shakespeare, which were not even, he observed, to be specially insured. The four-volume edition of Keats appeared in 1883; it contained two letters to Fanny Brawne previously unpub, lished. "From this mass of material," wrote a critic in *Mac, millan's Magazine*, "one section only could have been well spared; it is that which contains the letters to Fanny Brawne. Mr. Forman was originally responsible for publishing them, and is apparently impenitent."

The Lindons had given Mr. Forman three letters in recog, nition of his earlier work; one was still kept by Sir Charles; but about 1884, "owing to illness and some financial troubles,"[8] Margaret Lindon was obliged to sell the remaining thirty-five to a bookseller for a hundred pounds. In January 1885 it was announced in the press that "the original autograph letters addressed by John Keats to Miss Fanny Brawne . . . will be sold by Messrs. Sotheby, Wilkinson & Hodge in the first week in March."

The publication of the letters both Keats and Fanny Brawne had surmised and would have understood; the public auction of "Lot 1" on March 2nd, 1885, would have roused their deepest anger. The first letter, it is said, went to Oscar Wilde for £18; the letter in which Keats told Fanny that he was marking Spenser, was only "a short happy letter on one 8vo page," and fetched £9. The final heart-stricken message brought in £39, for, as "a most interesting but painful letter, evidently written in the greatest agony of mind," it had its commercial worth. The sale realized £543 17s., and was roundly and rightly condemned by *The Edinburgh Review* as "this act of desecration." That the Lindons were not directly responsible is beyond doubt; but adverse critics must have quoted the words attributed to Fanny, that "some day the letters would be considered of value."

The letters had been irretrievably scattered, and many of the originals are even now lost to sight. On June 14th, 1887, at Bon Air, Lausanne, there died at the age of seventy-eight the last of the innermost circle of those who used to meet at Elm Cottage and Wentworth Place. That day, and the following day, the announcement of her death appeared in the *Gazette de Lausanne*:

*M. et Mme Herbert Lindon et leurs enfants, Melle Marguerite Lindon, Mme Veuve Edmond Lindon et ses enfants, ont la douleur de faire part à leurs amis et connaissances du décès de*

Mme Marguerite
### PEREIRA DA CUNHA
*née Brawne,*

*leur tante et grand'tante, survenu mardi 14 juin, à 7 heures du matin. Le convoi funèbre partira de Bon-Air, jeudi 16 juin, à 5 heures. Culte à 4 h. ½.*

Margaret da Cunha left much of her money to the Free Church of the Canton of Vaud, for the widows of ministers, the propagation of the Gospel, and the mission to South Africa; to Margaret Lindon, Fanny's daughter, she bequeathed her jewellery, and among it was the quatrefoil amethyst brooch

which had been the gift of Keats. On June 16th, near the Lake
of Geneva, of which the poet had dreamed, the last of the
Brawne family was buried. On December 17th Fanny's son
changed his name to Brawne-Lindon.

In September 1889, Fred Holland Day wrote to Herbert
Lindon. A collector of Keatsiana, who had corresponded
with the Llanos, he may already have heard of Fanny Brawne's
thirty-one letters[9] to Keats's sister, and have thought even now
of their publication. He asked Herbert Lindon where Fanny
Brawne was buried and what had become of her miniature.
"My mother's grave," was the answer, "is not in St. George's
churchyard, as you rightly infer, but under any circumstances
I should have asked you not to carry out your intention of
publishing a photograph of it. No doubt her life, in so far as
it is connected with Keats, is more or less public property, but
I think that this ceased to be the case when she married, & I am
sure my father, with whom she is buried, would have wished
that what you propose should not be carried out. I have the
full face miniature to which you refer, but the same objection
applies to its publication."[10] Fanny Llanos died on December
16th, but the following year Holland Day met her family in
Madrid; he received the letters with permission to publish them
if either of the Lindons consented. If Herbert Lindon had read
them he would beyond doubt have insisted that they were
published, for they remain the finest vindication of Fanny
Brawne. The letters were not shown to him; and rebuffed by
silence or prohibition, Holland Day took them to Massachusetts, where they stayed for forty-three years.

Throughout the last decade of the century, the interest in
Keats steadily mounted. The Aldine edition of Keats, reprinted in 1891, had gone through six more editions by 1906;
and when, in 1891, Colvin refused to publish the letters to
Fanny Brawne, even *The Athenaeum* called him "uncomfortably

assertive in making a virtue of the omission." Interviews with members of the Hampstead circle became popular among literary men. Holland Day sought out Dr. Lord, who had been the Brawnes' physician and was now white-bearded and blind; with pleasure and inaccuracy Dr. Lord gave his reminiscences.[11] In May 1894, *The New Review* published an interview with Severn, which had been held, it was claimed, shortly before his death. The old man, resting his chin on his hand, and gazing duly "into the depths of that blue Italian sky" dismissed Fanny Brawne as "flighty and flirting"; he "had of course known of Keats's affection and semi-engagement. ... Poor Keats made terrible mistakes in the one affair to which his heart was given ... Bah! It was Lord and Lady Byron, Shelley and Harriet Westbrook over again. What riddles men are. ... What riddles! What riddles!" To William Graham, who claimed to have interviewed him, he read the final love-letter; and Graham, for the satisfaction of Victorian readers, reflected that Keats would have acted more to the purpose "had he sent the lady a box of chocolate creams and a dozen of gloves just half a size too small." This article, effectively faked, was reprinted in *The Literary World* and attacked immediately by Mrs. Perrins.[12]

### In Defence of Fanny Brawne

Dear Mr. Editor—

Poor Fanny Brawne! "Flighty and flirting": what a dreadful thing it is to be beloved by a genius! It seems as if people thought they could add to *his* merits by detracting from *hers*. I do not believe she was flighty, or she would not have become the clever, brilliant woman I remember; as to flirting I can't say, but Thackeray says, in the heading to one of her stories:

> "That other girls besides princesses
> Like to flirt, the author guesses."

But as Mr. Severn knew her so well, did *he* flirt with her? I am sure she was very much attached to Keats, as she had an illness when her engagement was broken off that nearly cost her her life.

The vigilant old lady had indeed become "one of the most interesting links with the literary London of the past, and to lovers of Hampstead her conversation had a singular charm."

A few weeks later, in July 1894, a bust of Keats was unveiled in Hampstead Parish Church; the ceremony was attended by a distinguished congregation including Lord Houghton, Sidney Colvin and, ironically, Professor Robinson Ellis, the son of the "downright Miss" who had once been Fanny's friend. In his speech Edmund Gosse remarked that "no one living today has seen John Keats"; a contradiction promptly appeared in the local paper:[13] "Keats, at the time of his death, was engaged to my cousin, Fanny Brawne. My elder brother John (now in his 87th year) . . . frequently conversed with John Keats." John Finch had long since published a criticism of Fanny; but it was now more profitable to acknowledge her. Nor were her cousins the only people to boast a connexion with her: Fred Holland Day, presenting the bust of Keats on behalf of America, could not resist referring to some letters in his keeping, "many of which are wholly devoted to [Keats] and his characteristics, written by no less a person than the lady whom he loved." It was, he emphasized, "in connection with Fanny Brawne that . . . the greatest misconceptions of him lay. These then in time must be cleared away, and I am confident that time will vindicate the man as it has already vindicated the Poet." It is one of the inexplicable facts of history that in the presence of the poet's biographers, a congregation of Keatsians and attentive journalists, the statement passed unnoticed.

"A certain fuss is being made in today's papers because yesterday was the centenary of Keats's birth." So said *The St. James's Gazette* on October 30th, 1895: "There was nothing peculiar," it continued, "about that very necessary ceremony; and it is no more important because yesterday was a hundred years since the poet was born, than because tomorrow makes a hundred years since the same interesting infant was two days old." The centenary was based on a common misunderstanding and did not, in fact, occur until October 31st; but the *Gazette* was not the only paper to display Victorian ignorance and pomposity. *The Daily Telegraph* saw fit to allude to "that extremely chilly and unresponsive young lady, Miss *Fanny Brawne*," and *The Standard*, sixteen years after the event, still regretted the publication of the letters. "In the chief love episode of his life . . . *Keats*, it must be acknowledged, was not so fortunate. . . . The object of his affections was hardly deserving of the amount of passion and lament he wasted on her. . . . The unreserved publication of those letters is a gross instance of that pandering to public curiosity which *Tennyson* has so rightly stigmatized."

Even so, Fanny Brawne retained some fascination, and another manufactured interview was supplied to meet the demand: in *The Century* for October there appeared the reminiscences of a nonagenarian who had sold papers to Keats. He professed to have known "Miss Fanny," and described the evening when he had gone to Wentworth Place "to ask after Mr. Keats. . . . I hadn't seen him for a long time tramping around. It was September, and the back door was half open, and just inside was Miss Brawne herself talking to one of the maids. I stammered out my words, not feeling sure of my welcome, someway. Her answer was curt enough, but I have always fancied she'd been crying. She said that Mr. Keats had that very morning gone to London to sail for Italy." The perfect timing of the visit, the absence of new details, and the presence of several striking inaccuracies did not escape the criticism of *The Hampstead and Highgate Express*; the editor inferred, and rightly, that the article had been "made in America."

In 1896, three-quarters of a century after the poet's death, a memorial plaque was unveiled on Lawn Bank, John Street,

Hampstead, the "unpretentious pleasant villa, stucco-fronted and discreetly gardened" which Keats and Fanny had known as Wentworth Place. The ceremony was witnessed by a few lovers of his poetry who even now misunderstood his life; and one of them, as he entered the house, still believed that from its windows Keats had "watched for his Charmian eighty years ago."

The nineteenth century, which had known the radiance of Keats, drew to its close; Fanny Brawne had entered history. There are some who recall her daughter, Margaret, in the early nineteen hundreds; she died in Lausanne on June 1st, 1907. Two years later, on October 6th, 1909, there died in Folkestone the last surviving child of Fanny Brawne; and to Herbert Lindon, who allowed the publication of her letters from Keats and gave their editor continual support, all who love literature must be grateful. In 1910, John Street, Hampstead, was re-named Keats Grove, and the following year, on the death of Sir Charles Dilke, his collection of relics was inherited by the Hampstead Borough Council. Early in 1920 there came into the market the unpretentious house known as Lawn Bank, and through the energy of the Mayor of Hampstead, a National Committee and admirers of the poet in the United States, it was bought and given to Hampstead to be maintained for ever; on May 9th, 1925, when it had been restored, it was opened to the public and called, once again, Wentworth Place. And after their pilgrimage of more than a century, to Waltham-stow and Pancras Lane, to Hampstead, France and Spain, to Italy and America, the letters of Fanny Brawne to Keats's sister returned at last in 1934, after the death of Holland Day, to the house in which they had been written. Three years later they were published.

# *Appendix*

## SOME RELATIONS AND ACQUAINTANCES OF
## FANNY BRAWNE

BELL, Mrs.

Fanny Brawne's "best dressmaker" probably took in sewing to augment the meagre income of her husband: Charles Bell of 62, Newman Street appears in the rate-books from 1822-1830, and *Robson* (1823) describes him as "a gold chaser."

BRAINE, John

The record of Old Westminsters includes John Braine, "eldest son of John Smith Braine, of H.M. Navy Office, Somerset House, London; born 2 June 1805; adm. 10 Jan. 1815; King's Scholar March 10, 1820; elected to Trinity College, Cambridge, 1823 (adm. pensioner May 9, 1823, scholar 1824); 12th Classic and 17th Junior Optime 1827; B.A. 1827; M.A. 1832; ordained; an Usher at the School 1826-1834; Master of a proprietary school at Stockwell, Surrey; died Sept. 26th 1848." From the book of Trinity matriculations and *The Gentleman's Magazine*, November 1848, come the minor details that he had been born at Stoke Damerel, Devonshire, and died at Buckfast Abbey. It has been suggested that the "George" mentioned in Mrs. Lindon's letter was the George T. Braine reported as bankrupt in 1847-1848. One might record that John's younger brother, Henry, also went to Westminster School and Trinity; and that one "J. W. Braine, esq. of St. James's-square" married Frances Amelia, daughter of "the late Olyett Woodhouse, esq. Advocate-General of Bombay," at St. James's, Westminster, in September 1832. The bride was a niece of Richard Woodhouse, Keats's friend.

BRAWNE, JANE (*Sister*)

Born December 21st, 1802, baptized January 31st, 1803, buried August 31st, 1803 (Ealing Parish Registers).

BRAWNE, JOHN (*Brother*)

Born February 11th, 1807, baptized March 25th (Hampstead Parish Registers). Among the Brawne papers at Keats House is a note of the burial of John Brown at St. Martin-in-the-Fields on August 28th, 1808. The same mis-spelling occurs elsewhere and can probably be discounted.

BRAWNE, Margaret, *later Mme da Cunha*

Born April 10th, 1809, at Hampstead, according to her marriage certificate, but on April 19th, according to her baptismal register and death certificate. Baptized at Hampstead on September 9th, 1818. Married João Antonio Pereira da Cunha at Dieppe on November 30th, 1833. After his retirement (1841) she seems to have lived for a while in Portugal. The Lausanne official bulletin for June 30th, 1887, contains a second announcement of her death.

BRAWNE, Samuel (*Father*)

The Will of Samuel Brawne. (Principal Probate Registry. Crickett, 160):

I Samuel Brawne of Kentish Town in the County of Middlesex, gentleman do make this my Last Will and Testament in the manner following, that is to say, I give and devise all that my Cottage, or Tene/ ment, Land and Heredits at Twyford in the County of Berks occupied as two Tenements and being copyhold of Inheritance and holden of the Manor of Hurst and also the kitchen garden occupied with Mrs Kent House being also copyhold unto my wife Frances Brawne for her life and after her decease I give and devise the same unto my son Samuel Brawne his heirs and assigns for ever. Also I give and bequeath unto my said wife All my household goods, furniture, plate, linen books and china for her own use and benefit. All the rest and residue of my estate and effects whatsoever which I have a power to dispose of I give, devise and bequeath unto my said wife, her heirs, Executors Advowsons and Assigns and I appoint her executrix of this my will. In witness whereof I have hereunto set my hand and seal this eleventh day of April 1810.

SAMUEL BRAWNE.

Proved on 14 April 1810.

The property at Twyford was eventually inherited by Fanny Brawne; as Mrs. Lindo, she sold it for £300 in June 1854. (Berkshire County Records, D/ENM 36, p. 296).

BRAWNE, Samuel (*Brother*)

Born July 26th, 1804, baptized September 2nd (Ealing Parish Registers). Among the Colvin papers at Keats House is a typewritten copy of notes by James Armitage Brown, the nephew of Charles Brown, in which he states: "I remember going to [Valentine Llanos'] chambers with a note from Samuel Brawne . . . he died of rapid consumption a year or two after Keats. I was at the same office with Brawne and sat at the same desk with him." Samuel's obituary appeared in *The Times* of March 29th, 1828: "*Died.* Yesterday morning, at the residence of his mother, Wentworth/place, Hampstead, Samuel, only surviving son of the late Samuel Brawne, Esq., in the 24th year of his age."

BROWN, Charles

Born in Lambeth in April 1787; died in New Zealand in June 1842. The close friend and biographer of Keats, he was also merchant, artist, dramatist, journalist and emigrant; he was partly responsible for building Wentworth Place and he remains a major figure in the Keats Circle. See *Some Letters and Miscellanea of Charles Brown*, edited by M. Buxton Forman (London, O.U.P., 1937); Sharp, *Life and Letters of Joseph Severn* (Sampson Low, Marston & Co., 1892); and biographical notes in Forman, pp. xlix et seq., and Rollins, I, liv et seq.

CORNISH, Mrs.

Possibly the wife of John Cornish, accountant and general agent of 22, Bread Street Hill (*Kent*, 1820, &c.), who might have been known professionally to Abbey.

CRESPIGNY, Caroline de

Daughter of Henry Bathurst (1744-1837), Bishop of Norwich, she was unhappily married to the Rev. H. de Crespigny. Among her works were *My Souvenir or Poems . . . with Translations etc.* (London and Heidelberg, 1844), and *A Vision of Great Men, with Other Poems and Translations from the Poetesses of Germany* (London and Heidelberg, 1848). In Medwin's *Nugae* (Heidelberg, 1848) there are translations from her poems and some of her original English verse. The archivist at Heidelberg, Dr. Derwein, has kindly sent me extracts from a contemporary diary in which Caroline de Crespigny, accompanied by her "oldest and most faithful slave, Captain Medwin," is pleasantly described. She excelled, writes the diarist, in playing the piano, harp and guitar, and though she was nearing fifty and her complexion was florid, she retained a certain beauty. She was said to be a former mistress of Byron's.

DA CUNHA, João Antonio Pereira, Chevalier (*Brother-in-law of Fanny*)

The future husband of Margaret Brawne was born at Benefica, near Lisbon, on October 12th, 1802. He was Comptroller to the Empress Dona Leopoldina of Habsburg before being appointed to the Brazilian Ministry of Foreign Affairs. He became Secretary to the Embassy Extraordinary to the Court of Lisbon on April 16th, 1826, and the following month he was transferred to the Brazilian Legation in London. On October 18th he was accredited Chargé d'Affaires during the absence of the Minister, and in November 1827 he became Chargé d'Affaires in Paris. On June 16th, 1828, he was transferred to Berlin, where he remained until the Mission was closed in 1830. For a time he lived in the Rue de la Ferme des Mathurins in Paris, but in 1833, at the time of his marriage, his address was given as 95, Rue de la Barre, Dieppe. On May 24th, 1836, he was appointed Resident Minister to Vienna; the da Cunhas arrived in Vienna at the end of November, and here they remained until da Cunha's retirement on October 11th, 1841. He had died by November 1883.

### DAVENPORT family

Friends of the Keats family and of Fanny Brawne. Davenport, whose Christian name has been given variously as Benjamin, Burrage and Burridge, is recorded in 1815 as a merchant at 46, Lime Street, and in 1817 at 2 (later 3), Dunster Court, Mincing Lane; from 1831 D. Davenport is given in his place. Burridge Davenport lived at 2, Church Row, Hampstead, as early as 1816, but appears in the court guide in *Robson*, 1840, at 11, Russell Place, Fitzroy Square; later he moved to Fulham. His descendants lived in Hampstead until the end of the century, when the house, the largest and perhaps the finest in Church Row, was demolished by Victorian town-planners. (A drawing of it was published in Barratt's *Annals of Hampstead*.)

### FINCH, Mary (*Aunt*) and her family

Mary Ricketts had married John Finch by 1807 and was living in Woburn Place as late as 1835. There were at least two children of the marriage: John Finch, junior (b. 1808) was, I think, responsible for the criticism of Fanny Brawne published by Colvin; he seems to have been a lawyer at Furnival's Inn. He was too ill to attend the unveiling of the Keats bust in 1894 and Holland Day, who tried to interview him, received a discouraging letter from John's younger brother. Arthur Elley Finch was then living at 30, Steele's Road, Haverstock Hill; he took an active interest in local history, writing to the *Highgate Express* on Keats, Fanny Brawne, and Johnson's School (July 25th, 1894), and on Sir Henry Vane (November 28th). He was also responsible for such publications as *Civilization: a sketch of its rise and progress; its modern safeguards and future prospects, etc.* (1876); *The Influence of Astronomical Discovery in the Development of the Human Mind* (1877); and *Witchcraft, conjuration, exorcism, and other assumed dealings with the devil, etc.* (1887). I am told that a Miss Finch, an artist in water-colours, and another relation of Fanny Brawne, was living in Steele's Road before the First World War.

### Goss family

John William Goss lived in Marsh Street, Walthamstow, as early as 1808, and later moved to Clay Street; as a churchwarden and an overseer of the poor he frequently worked with his neighbour Richard Abbey, and in London he served with Abbey on the Court of Common Council. *Johnston*, 1818, includes Goss, Whitehurst & Co., Bull Wharf, in the list of merchants; by 1821 Goss had gone into partnership with his son John William, and within three years the son took control of the business. Goss himself died before 1832. His wife, Bella, is recorded in the archives at Walthamstow; of their daughters, Sarah married Thomas Cuvelje, Margaret married John Skilbeck, and Agnes married George Beale Brown. She died two days before Samuel Brawne, and there is a plaque to her memory in Walthamstow church; her death was announced in *The Times* of March 29th, 1828.

GOULD, Margaret (*Aunt*) and her family
Margaret Ricketts married John Gould "of Isleworth in the County of Middlesex, Callico printer," at St. George's, Bloomsbury, in June 1808. (See *The Times*, June 16th, 1808.) There was at least one son, Edward, of the marriage. In the churchwarden's account book in Hampton, a Mr. Gould is recorded as a ratepayer from 1820-1826, when the entry is "Mr. Gould or occupier." *Pigot*, 1826-1827, still records John Gould among the gentry of Hampton, and he is recorded there as late as 1828-1829; he signed Fanny Brawne's marriage register in 1833. In an indenture of lease dated October 1835 (Middlesex County Records, 1835/8/524) he is described as "late of Isleworth but then residing at Bruges in the Kingdom of Belgium, Gentleman."

HENDERSON, Mrs.
Possibly the wife of Edward Henderson who lived next door to the chapel in Walthamstow; but *Robson* (1820) records a tailor, William Henderson, living at 13, Cherry Garden Stairs (Street?), Bermondsey, and it may be noted that *Critchett and Woods* (1821) mentions Rowcroft & Co. in the same small street. Henderson had moved from Bermondsey by 1827.

INHAMBUPÈ, Marquis de
Dr. Antônio Luiz Pereira da Cunha, later Marquis de Inhambupé, the father-in-law of Margaret Brawne, was born in Baía on April 6th, 1760, graduated as a Bachelor of Laws at Coimbra University and began a judicial career in Portugal. He was interim governor of the provinces of Baía and Pernambuco (1799-1802), Chancellor of the Appeal Court of Baía (1808) and Financial Counsellor in Rio de Janeiro (1815); supporting Brazil's declaration of independence, he helped to draw up the Constitution of the Brazilian Empire and he became, successively, a deputy in the Constituent Assembly, Senator for Pernambuco and, in 1825, Minister of Finance and Foreign Affairs. In this last capacity he signed with Great Britain the Treaty of 1826 which ended the slave trade from Africa. At his death, on September 18th, 1837, he was President of the Senate.
He had married Dona Maria Joaquina da Rocha, who died on March 2nd, 1861; there were, besides the Chevalier da Cunha, four children of the marriage: Dr. Lourenço de Assís Pereira da Cunha

(Counsellor, Professor of the Faculty of Medicine in Rio de Janeiro and Court Physician); Manuel Luiz Pereira da Cunha (an admiral); Dona Mariana Pereira da Cunha, and Dona Maria Benedita da Cunha.

### LANCASTER family

William Norton Lancaster and his wife Mary, the parents of 15 children, lived in Walthamstow as early as 1802, and their son Samuel was recorded there in the latter part of the century. In 1811 the Lancasters were in Clay Street, and here, in 1823, Mrs. Lancaster died prematurely. In 1826/1827 Lancaster lived in Marsh Street, near the Abbeys, while in 1832 his address was given as Eagle House, Marsh Street. In 1814, Lancaster, Goss and Abbey served together on the vestry. Lancaster is recorded as an insurance broker in Tokenhouse Yard in 1802, and as a merchant at New City Chambers or Lloyd's Coffee House in 1808, while in 1809 he worked at 8, over the Royal Exchange; he apparently retired after 1834.

### LORD, Dr. Charles

Born in 1804, the son of a rector, Charles Lord trained in medicine at the united hospitals of Guy's and St. Thomas's. He qualified in 1826 and the following year he became the partner of Dr. Rodd in Hampstead. Lord was a Poor Law medical officer and published a pamphlet on Poor Law medical relief. He was known for his independence and for his excellent conversation which, we are told, was enforced by "many classical and scriptural quotations"; he was a man of "undoubted ability, though somewhat difficult of temper." For his report on the public health of Hampstead, see Baines, pp. 129 et seq.; for obituary notices, see *The Hampstead and Highgate Express*, July 25th, 1891 and January 2nd, 1892.

### MORGAN. MRS. (*Fanny Brawne's dressmaker*)

In *Holden's Triennial Dictionary* for 1809/10/11, Mary Morgan, milliner and dressmaker, is recorded at 33, St. James's Street; she paid rates at 37, St. James's Place from 1811/1825, and in 1823/1824, as Miss Morgan, she appears in *Pigot's* list of milliners. In the list of private addresses for 1811, her namesakes are recorded at 68, Park Street, and 39, Southampton Buildings, Holborn.

### RICHARDSON, "The three Miss Richardsons"

Possibly related to Fanny through her grandmother, Jane Brawne, *née* Richardson; it is worth noting that James Richardson, of St. Leonard's Hill, Windsor, surrendered the Twyford property to Samuel Brawne the coachmaster in 1783, and that Fanny's marriage register was signed by A. Richardson, the Ann Richardson who lived at 3, Middlesex Place until Michaelmas 1833. Joseph Richardson had been recorded at that address since 1829.

RICKETTS family

Sir Sidney Colvin in *John Keats: His Life and Poetry, His Friends, Critics and After-Fame* (3rd edition, 1920) states that Mrs. Brawne was "a lady of West Indian connexions." These may have been among the following members of the Ricketts family mentioned in *The Gentleman's Magazine*, 1789-1816:

1789    Miss R., daughter of William Henry R., of Longwood, Hants, marries Lord Rosehill.

1790    Edward Jervis R., nephew of Sir John Jervis, K.B. (later Viscount St. Vincent) marries the daughter of Lord Saye and Sele.

1793    George Poyntz R., appointed Captain-General and Governor-in-Chief of Tobago.

1794    Appointed Captain-General and Governor-in-Chief of Barbados.

1798    William Henry R., a member of the Jamaican council, and late of Longwood, Hants, dies in Jamaica.

1800    George Poyntz R. dies. He was "in all respects a very superior character. His unsullied integrity, zeal, and ability, in the discharge of his public duties, had highly and justly endeared him to the colony he commanded. . . . His mild temper, enlightened benevolence, and fascinating manners, are deeply and permanently impressed on the hearts of his numerous and respectable connexions; and his nearest relatives will in time feel, as the noblest consolation, that nothing could exceed the rectitude of his life but the Christian fortitude which soothed its decline and dignified its close."

1801    Earl of St. Vincent created a viscount "with remainders severally and successively to William-Henry R., esq., captain in the royal navy, and the heirs male of his body lawfully begotten; to Edward Jervis R., Esq., barrister-at-law, brother of the said William Henry R., and sons of Mary R., by William-Henry R. esq. late of the island of Jamaica, deceased, and sister to the said John, Earl of St. Vincent."

1811    Death of George Crawford R., "late of Jamaica, and for many years Attorney-General and Advocate-General there."

1816    Death of G. P. R., "eldest son of the late G.P.R., esq., governor of Barbados, and cousin of the Earl of Liverpool."

The Earl of St. Vincent writes (1951): "I was recently given a photograph of a portrait on the back of which was written 'portrait of William Ricketts, son of Col. Thomas Richards, a gallant soldier in the army of Charles I. . . . William accompanied the expedition to Jamaica under Penn and Venables and was present at the conquest of Jamaica in 1655.

His commission being made out in the name of Ricketts, his descendants have borne that name ever since."

RICKETTS, John (*Grandfather*)

From his will, June 30th, 1809: "I John Ricketts of Richmond Place East Street Walworth in the County of Surry and also of Pruins [?] Crescent Margate in the County of Kent Gentleman . . . desire to be . . . privately buried in the Church Yard belonging to the Parish of St. John the Baptist Margate in the County of Kent without any funeral pomp and at as little expense as may be." Among his bequests to his daughter, Frances, "now the wife of Samuel Brawne of Kentish Town Gentleman" are the "rents issues and profits" of property in Deptford, Charles Street, Charles Court, West Smithfield &c. After her death these are to remain on trust for her children.

John Ricketts' obituary appeared in *The Times* on September 26th, 1809: "On the 16th. inst. at Margate, in the 63rd. year of his age, John Ricketts, Esq. of Walworth." He had remarried about 1801, his second wife being a widow, Martha Aslin, who inherited much of his property but died within a few months of him.

RICKETTS, John (*Uncle*)

From his will, proved on April 9th, 1816: "I give and bequeath unto my three Sisters Frances Brawne widow of Samuel Vernon Brawne deceased, Mary the wife of John Finch and Margaret the wife of John Gould one thousand one hundred pounds sterling cash." He leaves £1,500 on trust to be invested "as hereinafter mentioned unto and amongst my Nephew and Nieces Samuel Brawne Frances Brawne and Margaret Brawne . . . in the following shares and proportions two third parts thereof the whole into three equal parts being divided unto my said nephew . . . one moiety of the remaining third part thereof unto my said niece Frances Brawne [the other to Margaret Brawne] the respective portions . . . payable as and when they shall respectively attain their ages of twenty-one." In the meantime the trustees are to invest the money in one of the public funds or other Government securities on their behalf, the interest and dividends to be paid to Mrs. Brawne "for their main-tenance and Education so long as she shall continue to maintain and educate them." The trustees shall, when Samuel Brawne "is of an age to be placed out in Business raise and pay out of the residue of my estate and Effects [up to £200] as an Apprentice or Clerk's fee or otherwise for his advancement in the world." John Ricketts leaves all the plate hitherto unspecified to his sisters; it is to be divided into three equal shares, and they are to choose their own in order of age. All the property which has not been mentioned is to be sold, the proceeds to be given to

Mrs. Brawne or her assigns and after her death to be invested for her children with benefit of survivorship.

For the subsequent history of John Ricketts' property in Cross Street (St. Andrew, Holborn) in which Fanny Brawne had an interest, see the Indenture of Lease and of Appointment and Release, in the Middlesex County Records Office (1835/8/524).

John Ricketts died at Stoke Newington on April 5th, 1816, and was buried on April 14th at St. Paul's, Deptford.

RICKETTS, Lucy (*Aunt*)

In *The Gentleman's Magazine*, May 1802: *Obituary, with Anecdotes, of Remarkable Persons*, there is the entry: "April 6. At her father's house in Surrey-place, Kent road, of a decline, Miss Lucy Ricketts." She was buried at St. Paul's, Deptford, on April 12th.

ROBINSON, Caroline

Caroline Robinson was described in some detail by Keats at the end of 1818. She married James Ellis, "a landowner with large interests in the hop trade, and at one time a man of considerable fortune," and their son, Robinson Ellis, was born at Barming, Kent, on September 5th, 1834. On his entry to Rugby in 1850 he was registered as the "third son of the late James Ellis, Esq., Stoke, near Devonport." The later life of his mother cannot be traced, but Robinson Ellis when he died in 1913 was "one of the greatest Latin scholars of his time," and those who wrote his obituaries remembered that he was "the son of a lady friend of Fanny Brawne's, Keats's sweetheart."

RODD, Dr., and his family

George Ramsay Rodd, surgeon and accoucheur, is recorded in Hamp-stead in 1817, though he may have lived in the neighbourhood somewhat earlier; his wife is said to have been "the dearest friend" of Fanny Brawne. Dr. Rodd is mentioned in 1823 as a member of the Royal College of Surgeons, and in 1827 he took as his partner the newly qualified Charles Lord; after 1829 he does not appear in the list of local doctors. His house in the High Street was burnt down, and the site is now occupied by Stamp's the chemist; but his daughter, born in 1820, remained in Hampstead until 1841, living at Chestnut House, now demolished, in Rosslyn Hill, and at the White House, at the bottom of Pond Street. As Mrs. Perrins she proved to be of some importance in the later history of Fanny Brawne.

ROMAY, Mr.

*The Gentleman's Magazine* for October 1815 recording the news from Spain, mentions that "Gen. Romay (first in command under Gen. Porlier) and his aide-de-camp escaped, and have come over to England."

In both Valentine Llanos's novels, *Don Esteban* (1825) and *Sandoval* (1826), Gen. Porlier plays a considerable part: it seems quite probable that Romay was known to the author.

## ROWCROFT family

In all probability that of Thomas Rowcroft, shipbroker, of 9, Lime Street, Fenchurch Street (*Lowndes*, 1794). Rowcroft became an insurance broker, wharfinger, sailmaker, and in 1804 an alderman. For the family's interest in Spanish affairs see the supplement to *The Gentleman's Magazine* for 1808, *The Times*, January 12th, 1819, and *The Aldermen of the City of London*, by Alfred B. Beaven (Eden Fisher, 1913). Before he went to Peru, Rowcroft had worked for some years at 68, Upper Thames Street, where he was a neighbour of Goss and Whitehurst.

## SEVERN, Joseph

Born in Hoxton in December 1793, awarded the Academy's gold medal for his painting *The Cave of Despair* in 1819. He went to Rome with Keats in 1820, and spent most of his long life, as a fashionable artist and as British Consul, in Italy. He is chiefly known for his devotion to Keats during the last months of the poet's life, and we owe him the account of the final days and some invaluable portraits. He himself died in Rome in August 1879 and was buried beside Keats. See Sharp, *Life and Letters of Joseph Severn*, and Forman, xlv, Rollins I, cxxix et seq.

## VERNON, Joseph

Captain Jesse, in his *Life of George Brummell* (1844), says that one of Jane Brawne's sisters married "Mr. Vernon, an actor." I assume that this was Joseph Vernon, the only actor of that name whom I find recorded at the time; he achieved some eminence, and the Brawnes would not have propagated the name unless they had been proud of the connexion. "Master Vernon" acted with Garrick in *Alfred*, a three-act masque, at Drury Lane on February 23rd, 1751; he later took the parts of Master Stephen (*Every Man in His Humour*), Lancelot (*Merchant of Venice*), Amiens (*As You Like It*), Lysander (*Midsummer Night's Dream*), Roderigo (*Othello*), Lorenzo (*Merchant of Venice*), and many rôles in light or minor plays. On November 20th, 1779, he played Autolycus in Garrick's version of *The Winter's Tale*, Mrs. Robinson taking the part of Perdita. The *Theatrical Biography* (1772) noted: "It is seldom found that a good actor is a good singer—Vernon stands an exception to that rule; for tho' he now lives in point of voice upon the echo of his former reputation, he was excellent in both—and did not too apparent a coxcombry eternally settle upon his features, there are many parts in Comedy that would receive force from his abilities." Autolycus was said to be one of his best parts. Mrs. Vernon played Helena in 1755, in Garrick's version of *A Midsummer Night's Dream*: "a new English Opera called the Fairies."

WHITEHURST family

Whitehurst and Izon, founders, are recorded at Bull Wharf, Queenhithe, as early as 1793, though in the following year their address is given as 16, St. Martin's-le-Grand. In 1795 they were brass and ironfounders at Bull Wharf and in 1809 Thomas Whitehurst, an ironmaster, appears there in his own right; the firm of Whitehurst, Moore and Guest, nail ironmongers, is recorded in 1821, and Whitehurst himself is mentioned as late as 1828; a Thomas Whitehurst, licensed victualler, is given as the ratepayer for the Sir John Barleycorn, Drury Lane, from 1831-1834.

WIGRAM family

Sir Robert Wigram of Walthamstow House had twenty-three children. Many details about the family are given in *The Gentleman's Magazine*; *Chronicles of Blackwall Yard*, Part I, by Henry Green and Robert Wigram (1881); in *Pioneer Shipowners* by Clement Jones (1935); and in biographical notes in the Central Public Library at Poplar. The Wigrams' life at Walthamstow is recorded in the twelfth official publication of the Walthamstow Antiquarian Society, *Some Walthamstow Houses* (1924), and in the churchwarden's accounts. Sir Robert Wigram, M.P. for Fowey from 1802-1806, was head of Reid's Brewery, and of Huldart's Rope Works, Chairman of the East India Docks and Principal of the Blackwall Shipbuilding Yard, and he placed some of his sons in these concerns: Edward became a partner in the brewery and William was described by Macaulay as "the most obstinate of the East India Directors." Octavius became a director of the Royal Exchange Assurance Company, James was raised to the Bench as Vice-Chancellor, and Joseph became the Bishop of Rochester. In 1842 Walthamstow House was converted into a preparatory school and in 1885 it became an orphanage.

## II

## CHARLES BROWN'S VALENTINE TO FANNY BRAWNE

The original manuscript of the Valentine is not known to exist; but Fanny Brawne used to repeat the verses to her children, and they were sent by her daughter to Mr. Forman, with the following letter:

4 Abingdon Villas, W.

15 March 1878.

Dear Mr. Forman,

Do you remember our speaking of a valentine which Mr. Brown once sent to Mama? I have been trying to recollect it but cannot do so entirely

—here is all I can piece together. As you are interested in all concerning her I thought you might like to see it.

With kind regards from Herbert,
Believe me,
Yours truly
Margaret Lindon.

### The Valentine

Whene'er we chance to meet
You know the reason why
You pass me in the street
And toss your head on high—

Because my walking stick
Is not a dandy twig,
Because my boots are thick,
Because I wear a wig.

Because you think my coat
Too often has been worn,
And the tie about my throat
Is at the corners torn.

(Then there is something which I have forgotten about his hat being shabby and about his gloves being in holes, and then—)

To see me thus equipped
What folly to be haughty!
Pray were you never whipped
At school for being naughty?—

III

MRS. LINDON'S STATEMENT TO MEDWIN

Published in *The Life of Percy Bysshe Shelley*
by Thomas Medwin (1847).

The authorship of this statement is clear from internal evidence; it is proved to be the work of Mrs. Lindon by the annotations in Medwin's own copy.

Having quoted a phrase from Robert Finch's account of the last days of Keats, Medwin discusses the effect of the *Quarterly* review: it was, he writes, "a mere unit, and not the last in the glass."

"I am fortunately enabled, from a most authentic source, to set this matter at rest—by the kind communication of a lady who knew him well, better indeed than any other individual out of his own family. To confirm the else solitary opinion of Mr. Dilke, she says:

"'I did not know Keats at the time the review appeared. It was published, if I remember rightly, in June 1818. However great his mortification might have been, he was not, I should say, of a character likely to have displayed it in the manner mentioned in Mrs. Shelley's Remains of her husband. Keats, soon after the appearance of the review in question, started on a walking expedition into the Highlands. From thence he was forced to return, in consequence of the illness of a brother, whose death a few months afterwards affected him strongly.'"

[Medwin discusses Keats's Shakespeare, evidently borrowed from Mrs. Lindon, and the miniature of Keats "of which I have a copy through the kindness of the lady who knew so well to appreciate his heart and genius." He then quotes further from Mrs. Lindon:]

"It was about this time [continues my kind correspondent], that I became acquainted with Keats. We met frequently at the house of a mutual friend, (not Leigh Hunt's,) but neither then nor afterwards did I see anything in his manner to give the idea that he was brooding over any secret grief or disappointment. His conversation was in the highest degree interesting, and his spirits good, excepting at moments when anxiety regarding his brother's health dejected them. His own illness, that commenced in January 1820, began from inflammation in the lungs, from cold. In coughing, he ruptured a blood-vessel. An hereditary tendency to consumption was aggravated by the excessive susceptibility of his temperament, for I never see those often quoted lines of Dryden, without thinking how exactly they applied to Keats:

'The fiery soul, that working out its way,
Fretted the pigmy body to decay.'

From the commencement of his malady, he was forbidden to write a line of poetry, and his failing health, joined to the uncertainty of his prospects, often threw him into deep melancholy.

"The letter, p. 295 of Shelley's Remains, from Mr. Finch, seems to be calculated to give a very false idea of Keats. That his sensibility was most acute, is true, and his passions were very strong, but not violent, if by that term, violence of temper is implied. His was no doubt suscep- tible, but his anger seemed rather to turn on himself than on others, and in moments of greatest irritation, it was only by a sort of savage des- pondency that he sometimes grieved and wounded his friends. Violence such as the letter describes, was quite foreign to his nature. For more than a twelvemonth before quitting England, I saw him every day, often witnessed his sufferings, both mental and bodily, and I do not hesitate to say, that he never could have addressed an unkind expression, much less a violent one, to any human being. During the last few months before leaving his native country, his mind underwent a fierce conflict; for whatever in moments of grief or disappointment he might say or think, his most ardent desire was to live to redeem his name from the obloquy cast upon it; nor was it till he knew his death inevitable, that he eagerly wished to die. Mr. Finch's letter goes on to say,—'Keats might be judged insane,'—I believe the fever that consumed him, might have brought on a temporary species of delirium, that made his friend Mr. Severn's task a painful one."

Medwin quotes from Keats's letter to Mrs. Brawne, "the only letter, I believe, which he sent from Italy"; and from Severn's letter to Mrs. Brawne of February 21st, 1821.

## IV

### MRS. LINDON'S LETTER TO MRS. DILKE, 1848

Among Fred Holland Day's papers at Harvard is a photograph of a fragmentary letter written by Mrs. Lindon, presumably to Mrs. Dilke. The original apparently consisted of four pages, the top half of the first two pages being torn away; in the middle of the fourth page Sir Charles Dilke wrote: "Signed Frances Lindon & dated Nov$^r$. 1848." Professor Rollins, who found the photographs, writes in the *Harvard Library Bulletin* (Vol. V, No. III, pp. 372-3): "Evidently both signature and date were missing when around 1889-90 Sir Charles permitted Day to make the photograph." The whereabouts of the original remain unknown; perhaps the missing part of the letter, if not the whole, was burnt with the other Keats papers (see p. 141 and Appendix VI). The following is the text as Professor Rollins gives it:

. . . for a visit . . . I am sorry M$^r$ Di[l]ke does not edit it. I often think I trace his hand in certain parts. It is a delightful paper & that I repeat whenever I get hold of it. Only think of Fanny Hoods quarrel with her Aunts and that neither you nor I can get hold of the cause. Perhaps it is about M$^{rs}$ Dore. Fanny, like most young people, would be very warm in defence of a friend. To do M$^{rs}$. Hood justice, I must say, when she defended M$^{rs}$. Dore . . . [page 2] you must not be surprised at M$^r$. Lindons mentioning the *"memoirs"*. He has a very imperfect idea of the real case. *Perhaps thinks his wife had an admirer, the more.* He never would have heard of it, had it not happened about seven or eight years ago, he noticed the portrait in your room; and asked who it was. As you hesitated in answering, he felt puzzled & I, to prevent awkward mistakes in future, when we got home explained as much as was necessary. As to Capt Medwin, when we first went to Heidelberg, he by [page 3] chance stumbled on the Shakespeare with Mr. Keats name written in it. As he is always on the hunt for literary prey, he occasionally asked me questions but it was not till Mrs Shelly's life of Shelly fell into my hands that we at all entered into the subject. I was much shocked at a letter written by a Mr Finch which she, very unnecessarily published. It gave an account of the last few weeks of poor Keats life that I wondered Mr Severn did not contradict. I shewed Captain Medwin the letter in my possession which gave such a different picture of what passed & he asked me to let him publish it. I was not aware that any *legal* objection existed or I should not have let him have it. There would be no other as it only does Mr. Severn credit & he has been anxious himself to bring it forward. As this is the case, & he must have guessed from whom the extract (it was no more) from his letter was obtained. I think that which he wrote to Capt. Medwin quite uncalled for. At the same time, I should be sorry for any ill feeling to exist between myself & Mr. Severn, whose kindness I have always appreciated.—so if you have an opportunity, you may just say, I am sorry I did not know of his *legal* rights. While on the subject I must tell you, I in no way brought *myself* in, to Captain Medn., but spoke of that letter and another as having been addressed to my mother, which they were. Altogether I [page 4] reflected afterwards whether it had seemed odd & that I might have given a strange impression of my Mothers having such an intimacy with a young man. But cunning Mrs. de Crespigny was not to be taken in, & asked Mr. Lindon, on his next visit, whether Mr. Keats had been an admirer of Mrs. Lindon's—and he, taken by surprise, knew just enough to answer yes. If Medwin had known that I possessed the Cenci by Shelly marked with many of Keats notes he would have been miserable till he got it, but I kept that and others out of his way. The greater part of his information he got out of the "Indicator" and perhaps from Shelly for he mentions several things I did not know myself.

Inspired by your journey to Boulogne, I wrote to Mrs. Robinson; a great exertion for me, as she owed me a letter. I am afraid, poor thing, she is in a very bad state of health. It is the same complaint that her mother died of. She mentioned your visit with great delight.

So John Braine is dead! He never succeeded in life as I expected, and it puzzles me. He had every requisite, talent, perseverance, impudence to push. Perhaps he was too selfish—yet that is the very thing some people get on by. I read in the paper that George had failed for £360,000, a very decent smash. It was mentioned that he had returned from India two years before with £200,000. Only think of . . .

Professor Rollins notes that Thomas Hood seems to have met the Lindo[n]s abroad.

Writing to Dilke about January 12th, 1836 (*Letters of Thomas Hood*, ed. L. A. Marchand, New Brunswick, N.J., 1945, p. 76), Hood says: "The Lindos are in fortune's round about too. She forgot part of her commission so we had a postscript package—containing the favour of your two packs of English cards." Mrs. Lindon may also be the "Mrs. L." Hood mentioned in an earlier letter of the same month: "By way of climax, think of Mrs. L. being detained nearly a fortnight with our letters at Rotterdam, because somebody in England had neglected to ship [her?] luggage." The name Lindo occurs more than once in Hood's verse, though evidently for the sake of the rhyme (see, for example, *Over the Way*, in *Hood's Own: or, Laughter from Year to Year*, 1839).

## V

## "A RELATIVE OF MRS. LINDON"

(Sharp, *Life and Letters of Joseph Severn*, 1892, pp. 283-4.)

The following letter, which may be dated 1883, was probably written by the daughter-in-law of Fanny Brawne: Mrs. Edmund Lindon. I think it was she who, "by a singular chance, ministered to Severn in his old age."

"I see by the *Italia* that you have arrived in Rome, with your father's old friend, Lord Houghton, for the touching ceremony of placing your father's remains near the friend of his youth, as he, too, had always expressed the wish for, as well as being surrounded with violets, a flower and perfume he delighted in. They and the rose were his favourite flowers, and often and often I have taken them to him when he was no longer able to go out and see them blooming in the gardens. . . . I have ordered my clerk, Signor Framminghi, to be the bearer of this note and to receive your wishes respecting the 'Souvenirs de Famille', which Signorina Margherita, Dr. Valeriani's sister, begged to give up to the different members of my kind old friend's family. . . . One of my first thoughts on returning home will be to place a wreath of violets on your dear father's *new* resting-place."

Among the unpublished letters at Keats House is one from Severn to his sister Maria in which he mentions a Mrs. Linder, Linden or, I think, Lindon (his handwriting in his old age is not clear):

"Rome, 24 Feby. 1874.

"On Xmas day I was invited to a splendid repast at my great fd. Mrs. Lindon's—a party of 10 and a most choice dinner—I went thro the fatigue bravely—this Lady most kindly takes me out in her fine carriage and is very attentive."

On June 23rd, 1877, he writes to his daughter Eleanor from Rome:

"I had thought of going to Olivone but Mrs. Lindon advised me to stay in Rome & not trust myself to the inconveniences of the country— This I have decided on."

## VI

## SIR CHARLES DILKE AND HIS KEATSIANA

Mr. Harry K. Hudson, private secretary to Sir Charles Dilke from 1887 to 1911, wrote to me in January 1951 that he had seen Sir Charles burn some of Keats's letters. It seems fair, however, to quote from Mr. Hudson's further letter: "If you think well you can say that I saw Sir Charles Dilke burn some Keats letters. But I'm not sure if it is wise to mention this. People may think there was something bad in the letters. I don't know what they were."

A letter from Mr. H. Buxton Forman to Sir Charles, which recently came to light, refers to some other Keatsiana which is unknown today; it was written on June 4th, 1890, after Mr. Forman had given a sub-stantial account of Fanny Brawne in the 1889 edition of the love-letters. "Of the character of Fanny Brawne [so Mr. Forman wrote], I formed a definite conception, from such documents and statements as were acces-sible to me . . . the passage you have been kind enough to send me ["the episode of Mr. Lindon and the portrait," apparently from the letter of 1848] fits in with my conception; but I cannot say what I might get to think if I saw the letters you mention in their entirety. At present, I am doing nothing fresh about Keats; but if, for example, I had to write his life, I should feel compelled to ask for a sight of those letters, in order to give myself a chance of revising the fundamental conception of her character."

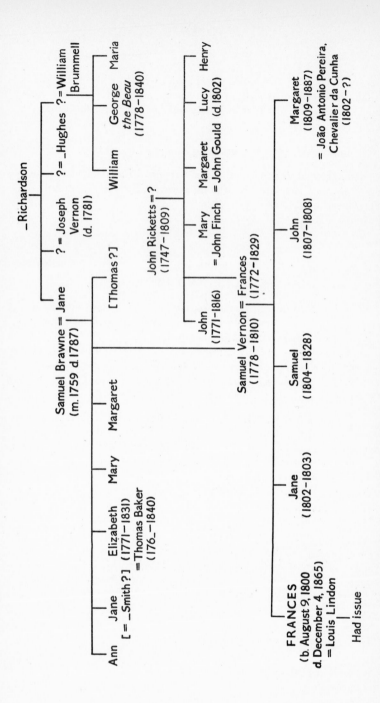

GENEALOGICAL TREE OF THE BRAWNE FAMILY

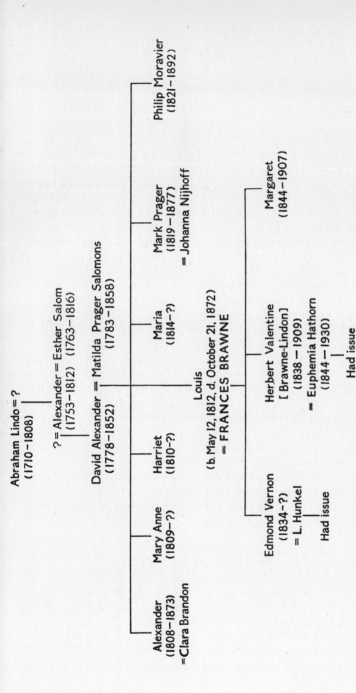

GENEALOGICAL TREE OF THE LINDON FAMILY

# Notes

## PROLOGUE

[1] In *The Life of George Brummell, Esq., commonly called Beau Brummell* (1844), Captain Jesse describes the marriage of Beau Brummell's mother; another of her sisters, he continues, "married Mr. Vernon, an actor; a third sister espoused a Mr. Hughes, a very respectable person in the City; and the fourth, married a gentleman of the name of Brawn, who had a farm near Lilbourn [*sic*].

"George Brummell occasionally paid a visit to his aunt Brawn; and one of the earliest episodes remembered of his childhood is, that he was one day guilty of crying most bitterly, because he could not eat any more of her ample damson tart."

[2] Rosa Perrins, *Recollections of Old Hampstead: The Hampstead Annual*, 1898, pp. 139-141.

[3] In *Keats's Publisher*, pp. 96 et seq., Edmund Blunden notes that Isabella Jones "writes—no date, but I think in 1818—inviting Taylor to a house-warming party at 57, Lamb's Conduit Street. A year later she sends another invitation and desires him to bring Reynolds." Her name does not appear in the rate-books for this period, and it seems possible that she rented rooms in James Rycutt's house, 34, Gloucester Street, towards the end of the year. The Hastings woman knew Reynolds and George Keats and, apparently, other members of the circle, while Mrs. Jones knew Reynolds and Taylor and possibly Brown. The books and music which Keats found in Gloucester Street suggest that the Hastings woman was cultured, while Mrs. Jones was eventually given one of Keats's books, which were not light reading. The Hastings acquaintance received visits from Keats at least until February 1819, and Mrs. Jones was still among his friends on his leaving England.

## KEATS AND FANNY BRAWNE

[1] Mrs. Oswald Ellis, quoted in *The Sphere*, May 16th, 1925.

[2] The book list is taken from the pencilled annotations in Fanny Brawne's *Literary Pocket Book*, now at Keats House.

[3] Mrs. Perrins in *The Hampstead and Highgate Express*, August 1894.

[4] Keats and Fanny both read Buffon and Molière; Keats's edition of the comedies may yet be identified by the duodecimo illustrations to *Le Dépit*

*Amoureux* and *La Critique de l'École des Femmes* which Fanny pasted into her scrapbook.

⁵ Fanny uses this phrase in reference to Byron, but in all probability she would have applied it to Keats.

⁶ Mrs. Lindon's statement in Medwin's *Life of Shelley* (1847).

⁷ She took special pains with her hair, wrote H. Buxton Forman in 1889, wearing it "in curls over the forehead, interlaced with ribands"; in the silhouette it is hanging in long curls on the nape of her neck, in the miniature it is parted in the centre and braided and coiled over her ears.

⁸ Letter of July 8th, 1819 (*Letters*, p. 357); Keats's love is also partly explained by his remark to Bailey, November 22nd, 1817 (p. 67): "I am certain of nothing but the holiness of the Heart's affections and the truth of Imagination—what the Imagination seizes as Beauty must be truth . . . for I have the same Idea of all our Passions as of Love they are all in their sublime, creative of essential Beauty."

⁹ Fanny Brawne's comment (Edgcumbe, p. 41) is the authority for this date; there seems no other explanation of her words nor of the joyous and inspired mood in which Keats began the new year.

¹⁰ "At Winchester I shall get your Letters more readily; and it being a cathedral City I shall have a pleasure always a great one to me when near a Cathedral, of reading them during the service up and down the Aisle." There may be a half-truth in Keats's light-hearted remark of August 5th, 1819 (Forman, p. 367); and possibly, at Chichester, he received a letter from Fanny. She kept no answer to it, but perhaps his reply was to write *The Eve of St. Agnes*.

¹¹ Reminiscences of John Finch, quoted by Colvin.

¹² Mrs. Perrins in *The Hampstead Annual*, 1898, pp. 139-141. See also *The Hampstead and Highgate Express*, August 1894: Mrs. Perrins states that Mrs. Brawne "and all her family were strongly opposed to the match, partly because of the poet's delicacy, and partly because they thought his genius a kind of mad craze."

¹³ Sharp, *Life of Severn*.

¹⁴ See Appendix II.

¹⁵ At the beginning of April, according to Brown (letter to Dilke in the Keats Museum), Keats had drawn £106 7s. 7d. "out of Abbey's hands, as of Account Current, being the remainder of the £500 and interest. A considerable portion of that sum . . . went . . . to pay bills; with the remainder he went to the Isle of Wight." Keats therefore had no ready capital when he left Hampstead.

¹⁶ Letter from Brown to Dilke in the Keats Museum.

¹⁷ There seems good reason to place this letter (Forman, pp. 496-7) before the one which is printed on pp. 490-1. Despite the order in which he has published them, Mr. Forman made this suggestion, and it is

supported by internal evidence. In the Wednesday letter Keats says that he will ask Mrs. Brawne whether Fanny has been to the Dilkes'; by the time he writes again he has heard of her visit to town. In the second letter he mentions writing to Fanny "yesterday": that might date his letters Wednesday and Thursday respectively. Keats was careless of dates and quite capable of writing Tuesday where Thursday would have been correct.

[18] *Lord Byron and His Contemporaries* (second edition, 1828), p. 439.

[19] *Table Book*, 1828, col. 249.

[20] Mrs. Perrins in *The Literary World*, May 11th, 1894.

[21] The note from Hunt is now at Keats House; it was evidently complete when Sir Charles Dilke printed it in *Papers of a Critic* (1875), but he appears to have cut out the reference to Fanny Brawne before he bequeathed the letter to Hampstead. The letter from the Olliers (see also p. 140) is also at Hampstead; so is the pocket-book. The copy of *Foliage* passed into the Buxton Forman collection, but I do not know where it is today. The Spenser was evidently seen by Monckton Milnes, and is presumed lost in Germany; it had been mislaid by 1872 (see p. 140). The pocket Dante is now in the Buxton Forman Collection (see Rollins, I, 254). In the letter of July 27th, 1820, in which Shelley invited Keats to Pisa, he remarked: "I always tell Ollier to send you copies of my books.— 'Prometheus Unbound' I imagine you will receive nearly at the same time with this letter. The Cenci I hope you have already received." *Prometheus Unbound* was omitted from the list of Keats's books, but *The Cenci* was included; its present whereabouts are unknown. The folio Shakespeare is at Hampstead, and in 1925 Mrs. Ellis presented a number of Brawne relics to the Museum, including Fanny's engagement ring from Keats, Margaret's brooch, and a piece of shantung silk which is quite probably a memento. The miniature (see pp. 137-8) is now in the National Portrait Gallery. As for the Etruscan lamp, it was once in the Buxton Forman collection and a picture of it was reproduced by Barratt in *The Annals of Hampstead* (1912), vol. II, p. 165; but though Keats may have given the lamp to Fanny Brawne, one cannot accept the statement that he had received it from Byron, whose dislike of him is only too well known.

[22] Rollins, *The Keats Circle*, vol. I, p. 170.

## THE YEARS AFTER

[1] H. Buxton Forman, Introduction to *Letters of John Keats to Fanny Brawne*, second edition, 1889, pp. lxv-lxvi.

[2] Mrs. Perrins in *The Literary World*, May 11th, 1894.

[3] H. Buxton Forman, op. cit.

[4] Brown to Severn, in letter quoted by Sharp, p. 109.

[5] Mrs. Perrins in *The Hampstead and Highgate Express*, August 1894: "Readers of *The Fortunes of Nigel* will remember that a great trouble has a similar effect on the Lady Hermione, the mysterious inmate of George Heriot's home. *The Fortunes of Nigel* appeared in 1822, when the circumstances of Keats's death were still fresh in mind. Scott, as we know, was in the way of hearing a good deal of Hampstead gossip. Could there be any connexion between Miss Brawne's case and that of Lady Dalgarno?"

[6] Severn saw a strong likeness to Fanny Brawne in the figure of Profane Love in Titian's *Sacred and Profane Love*; the picture is still in the Borghese Palace. See also Severn to Milnes, October 6th, 1845 (*Rollins*, II, p. 130), and to H. Buxton Forman, October 20th and 28th, 1877: *Letters of Joseph Severn to H. Buxton Forman* (Oxford. Printed for private circulation, 1933).

[7] See *The Times*, November 16th, 1932. The brooch is now at Keats House.

[8] This letter and the others published by Edgcumbe, pp. 52-58, may be more precisely dated. Edgcumbe ascribes Letter 21 (p. 52) to the summer of 1822, a general date which may be accepted; but we learn from this letter that the Romays will leave Hampstead "next Sunday, the 8th." The only summer month in 1822 in which the 8th fell on a Sunday was September. It therefore seems that this letter, finished on the Monday before the Romays' departure, was finished on September 2nd, and that Fanny had returned from Hampton on August 29th. If she spent, as she says, three weeks with her aunt, we may date her departure from Hampstead August 8th. Letter 23 (pp. 57-58), apparently from Wentworth Place, was headed "Saturday Morn" and postmarked in August and must have been written on August 3rd. Letter 22 is headed "Friday" and probably belongs to September 13th.

[9] Now at Keats House.

[10] "Thackeray says, in the heading to one of her stories:

> That other girls besides princesses
> Like to flirt, the author guesses."

Mrs. Perrins in *The Literary World*, May 11th, 1894. This couplet does not introduce any story in *Blackwood's* between 1820 and 1865. The manuscript of *Nickel List* is in the British Museum, and was published by M. Buxton Forman in *Blackwood's* in 1942.

[11] This and the following letter were published in the Buxton Forman edition of Keats (1883), vol. IV.

[12] Holland Day to Miss Lowell, March 13th, 1921: Rollins, *Keats and the Bostonians* (1951), p. 104.

[13] Mrs. Perrins in *The Hampstead and Highgate Express*, August 1894.

Mrs. Perrins, added the journalist who interviewed her, "is a firm believer in the sincerity both of Keats and of Fanny; and thinks that if Keats had to say at last, 'The thought of leaving Miss Brawne is beyond every thing horrible . . .' the fault was with circumstances and not with her."

[14] Marie Adami, *Fanny Keats*, p. 133.

[15] See Holland Day's account of his conversation with Lord in 1890 (Harvard); but according to *The Sphere*, May 16th, 1925, Mrs. Ellis was often told by her father, Herbert Lindon, that Fanny Brawne wore mourning for three years.

[16] Mrs. Perrins in *The Hampstead Annual*, 1898, pp. 139-41; and in *The Hampstead and Highgate Express*, August 1894.

[17] See Holland Day's account of his conversation with Lord; Dilke's letter is in the Keats-Shelley Memorial House in Rome.

[18] The Lindons to H. Buxton Forman, quoted in *Letters of John Keats to Fanny Brawne*, 1889.

[19] Entry in the Edgcumbe note-book at Keats House.

[20] At this point in the draft letter Fanny wrote: "I was more generous ten years ago, I should not now endure the odium of being connected with one who was working up his way against poverty and evry sort of abuse." As she crossed out this sentence, it is not given in the text. It suggests the prolonged strain which she had felt during her engagement, and the emotional disturbance caused by her mother's recent death, but it is no evidence of a final change of heart.

[21] Adami, p. 133.

[22] "Soon after 1830" according to Mr. Blunden in *Keats's Publisher*, p. 191. ("Life and Letters Series," Cape, 1940.)

[23] Verbal statement from Mrs. Ellis to the author, December 1950.

[24] Adami, p. 137.

[25] This and the following impressions of Viennese life were recorded in Clara Novello's *Reminiscences*, compiled by her daughter (1910), pp. 74 et seq.

[26] Mrs. Perrins in *The Hampstead and Highgate Express*, August 1894.

[27] The Lindons' travels remain largely a series of speculations and probabilities; but Edgcumbe, introducing Fanny Brawne's *Letters*, says that her scrapbook was a record of her tours, and in her book (now at Keats House) Budapest and Prague are well represented.

[28] Mrs. Ellis in *The Sphere*, May 16th, 1925.

[29] ibid.

[30] Verbal statement from Mrs. Ellis to the author, December 1950.

[31] Mr. Forman writes, in his edition of Keats's *Letters* (1942), p. lix, that "the statement concerning Lindon's connexion with the Exhibition [of 1851] fails of verification today. I feel sure that his son imparted the information to my father in the course of conversation." Dilke's son was

a member of the Executive Committee of the Great Exhibition in 1851 and, according to the official record, took charge of the correspondence and was the general superintendent. The heavy routine clerical work, which continued for more than two years, required a number of secretaries who were prepared to accept responsibilities and able to read and write other languages; and if Louis Lindon were concerned with the first Exhibition, this would surely have been his occupation. In no list of officials does his name appear, but the younger Dilke would have welcomed an assistant who was not only the husband of Fanny Brawne but spoke fluent French and German and probably Dutch and Spanish. It may be that Louis Lindon worked abroad, for he does not appear in the London directory for 1851. It seems more probable, however, that he was concerned with the Exhibition of 1862, for by that time he had settled in London with his family. Mrs. Ellis told the author in December 1950 that Herbert Lindon made a plan of one Exhibition for the authorities, a performance which seems more likely from a young man of twenty-four than from a schoolboy of thirteen; there is, besides, her statement, recorded at Keats House, that the family came back to England when he was twenty-one, a fact which would date their return 1859.

[32] On his wife's death certificate, Louis Lindon's occupation is given as "wine merchant's clerk."

### EPILOGUE

[1] See Appendix VI.

[2] Holland Day records in the Harvard typescript that when Mr. Forman first knew Herbert Lindon, neither of them was well-to-do and that Forman could not afford to buy the letters. Through Forman's influence, however, they were bought by a dealer in Piccadilly who let him publish them for a consideration. When Herbert Lindon heard that the letters would be auctioned, he tried to buy them back from Forman, but they had passed from their editor's control.

[3] Unpublished letter from H. Buxton Forman to Fanny Llanos, now at Keats House.

[4] *Letters of Joseph Severn to H. Buxton Forman.* (Oxford. Printed for private circulation, 1933.)

[5] Unpublished letter (now at Keats House) to his sister Maria, December 9th, 1877.

[6] In *Notes and Queries*, Fifth Series, IX, March 2nd, 1878.

[7] Introduction to *The Keats Letters, Papers and Other Relics forming the Dilke Bequest, etc.* (Lane, 1914).

[8] Statement authorised by Mrs. Ellis.

[9] The history of these letters is excellently told by Professor Rollins in *Keats and the Bostonians* (Harvard. London: Geoffrey Cumberlege, 1951).

[10] Original letter at Harvard.

[11] Dr. Lord told Day in 1890 that the Brawnes had moved from Hampstead before 1827 and had settled in Paddington; talking of Hampstead he added that Elm Cottage stood at the bottom of Pond Street and was (in 1890) a tea-house. The following extracts come from his letter on Keats which was published in *The Hampstead and Highgate Express* on July 26th: "Some cousins of the famed poet, living in America, recently desired to publish a full memoir of him, and sought for material, especially in Hampstead. It had transpired that many of Keats's affec-tionate letters to Fanny were written from Elm Cottage [*sic*], whence he looked across to the garden in the rear of Mrs. Brawne's house. . . . I was then living in Elm Cottage, Rosslyn Hill; but from this house it was impossible for Keats to have looked on the garden of Mrs. Brawne. . . . I mentally reviewed the district as it was before 1830, bringing to mind . . . the two pretty villa-cottages extending towards the road leading to Picketts' Dairy. Nearly opposite the last house in the row was a stately elm, with rough broad seat, and it suddenly flashed across my mind that this was the house and elm tree the Americans were in search of. I had in early days visited the widow of the Rev. Dr. Town, then lodging in this little cottage (now used for tea-taking visitors). It must have been here in former years that Keats had written so ardently and looked so tenderly across to the dwelling of Miss Brawne." I quote this as a pleasant example of misguided information. It may be worth mentioning that Elm Cottage, West End, Hampstead, a "small" detached cottage with seven bedrooms and "neat garden," was advertised in *The Times* on March 19th, 1822; but if, as Dilke recorded (and most Keatsians believe), Mrs. Brawne took a house "at the top of Downshire Hill," it would have stood on the corner of Rosslyn Hill, and must have been the cottage in which Lord himself had lived.

[12] The Severn interview was reprinted as "Fanny Brawne Again" in *The Literary World*, May 4th, 1894; Mrs. Perrins's reply, "In Defence of Fanny Brawne," appeared in the following issue, on May 11th.

[13] *The Hampstead and Highgate Express*, July 25th, 1894.

# Bibliography

THROUGHOUT this biography the text of Keats's letters is that of Mr. Maurice Buxton Forman's edition (O.U.P., 1942); the text of Keats's poetry is generally that recorded in his letters or given in Professor H.W. Garrod's edition of the *Poetical Works* (Oxford: Clarendon Press, 1939). The letters of Fanny Brawne are taken from the Oxford Bookshelf version, edited by the late Mr. Fred Edgcumbe (O.U.P., 1937), and from the biographical sketch in the volume of Keats's letters and the Holland Day papers in the Houghton Library of Harvard University. I have retained the punctuation and spelling of these texts as far as seemed practical, and for any omissions or changes I must take responsibility. I have not listed the numerous directories used, nor the majority of the periodicals, but most of the comments from the Victorian press have been found in the Potter Collection at Keats House and in the archives of the Hampstead Central Public Library. The following books, among others, have been consulted:

Adami, Marie. *Fanny Keats* (Murray, 1937).

Adams, Mary. *Some Hampstead Memories* (Priory Press, Hampstead, 1909).

Arnold, Matthew. *Essays in Criticism*, 2nd series (Macmillan, 1888).

Baines, F. E. (ed.). *Records of the Manor, Parish, and Borough of Hampstead* (Whittaker & Co., 1890).

Barratt, Thomas J. *The Annals of Hampstead* (A. & C. Black, 1912).

Beaven, Alfred B. *The Aldermen of the City of London* (Eden Fisher, 1913).

Birkenhead, Sheila. *Against Oblivion: the Life of Joseph Severn* (Cassell, 1943).

*Blackwood's Magazine.*

Blunden, Edmund. *Keats's Publisher: a Memoir of John Taylor* (Cape, 1936).

Blunden, Edmund. *Leigh Hunt* (Cobden-Sanderson, 1930).

Caine, T. Hall. *Recollections of Dante Gabriel Rossetti* (Elliot Stock, 1882).

Chancellor, E. Beresford. *History of the Squares of London* (Kegan Paul, 1907).

Colvin, Sidney. *Keats* ("English Men of Letters," Macmillan, 1887 and 1889).

Colvin, Sidney. *John Keats: His Life and Poetry, His Friends, Critics and After-Fame* (3rd edition, Macmillan, 1920).

Cowden Clarke, Charles and Mary. *Recollections of Writers* (2nd edition, 1878).

Denyer, C. H. (ed.). *St. Pancras through the Centuries* (Le Play House Press, 1935).

Dilke, Sir Charles Wentworth, Bart., M.P. *The Papers of a Critic, selected from the writings of the late Charles Wentworth Dilke* (Murray, 1875).

Dugdale, Sir William. *The Antiquities of Warwickshire* (1730).

Evans, B. Ifor. *Keats* ("Great Lives" Series, Duckworth, 1934).

Forman, Harry Buxton (ed.). Works of Keats, 1883, etc.

Forman, Harry Buxton (ed.). *The Life of Percy Bysshe Shelley, by Medwin* (O.U.P. 1913).

Forman, Maurice Buxton (ed.). *Some Letters and Miscellanea of Charles Brown* (London, O.U.P., 1937).

Garrod, H.W. *Keats* (O.U.P., 1926).

Genest, John. *Some Account of the English stage from the Restoration in 1660 to 1830* (Carrington, Bath, 1832).

*Gentleman's Magazine, The.*

Griffin, Daniel, *Life of Gerald Griffin* (1843).

*Hampstead Annual, The.*

Hampstead Antiquarian and Historical Society. Transactions for 1898.

Hewlett, Dorothy. *A Life of John Keats* (Hurst & Blackett, 1948).

Hill, Mary. *Hampstead in Light and Shade* (Bale, 1938).

Hone, William. *Every-Day Book*, 1826 and 1827.

Hone, William. *Table Book*, 1828.

Houghton, Lord (ed.). *The Poetical Works of John Keats* (Aldine edition, Bell, 1876).

Howitt, Mary. *An Autobiography*, edited by Margaret Howitt (Isbister, 1889).

Howitt, William. *Homes and Haunts of the Most Eminent British Poets* (Richard Bentley, 1847).

Howitt, William. *The Northern Heights of London* (Longmans, Green, 1869).

Hunt, James Henry Leigh. *The Literary Pocket-Book*, 1819.

Hunt, James Henry Leigh. *Lord Byron and some of his Contemporaries* (2nd edition, Henry Colburn, 1828).

Hunt, James Henry Leigh. *Imagination and Fancy* (Smith, Elder & Co. 1844).

Ingpen, Roger (ed.). *The Letters of Percy Bysshe Shelley* (Bell, 1914).
International Exhibition, 1862; Official Illustrated Catalogue.

Jackson, Mrs. F. Nevill. *Ancestors in Silhouette cut by Auguste Edouart. Illustrative Notes and Biographical Sketches* (John Lane, The Bodley Head, 1921 (?)).
Jesse, Captain W. *The Life of George Brummell, Esq., commonly called Beau Brummell* (Saunders & Otley, 1844).
*Jewish Encyclopaedia, The* (Funk and Wagnalls, 1925).

*Keats, John: The Poetical Works of.* With a Life by James R. Lowell (Boston. Little, Brown, 1854).

Llanos, Fanny Keats de, and H. Buxton Forman. Correspondence.
Lysons, Daniel. *The Environs of London* (1795).

Marchand, L. A. (ed.). *Letters of Thomas Hood* (New Brunswick, N.J., 1945).
Maxwell, Anna. *Hampstead, its Historic Houses, its Literary and Artistic Associations* (James Clarke, 1912).
Medwin, Thomas. *The Life of Percy Bysshe Shelley* (1847).
Milnes, Richard Monckton (later Lord Houghton). *Life, Letters and Literary Remains of John Keats* (Moxon, 1848).
Moya, Salvador de. *Anvario Genealógico Brasileiro* (São Paulo, 1941).
Murry, John Middleton. *Keats and Shakespeare* (O.U.P., 1926).

*Nieuw Nederlandsch Biografisch Wordenboek* (Leiden, 1914 and 1930).
Nitichie, Elizabeth. *The Reverend Colonel Finch* (Columbia University Press, New York, 1940).
Novello, Clara. *Reminiscences.* Compiled by Contessa Valeria Gigliucci (Arnold, 1910).

Palmer, Samuel. *St. Pancras* (Samuel Palmer, 1870).
Park, J. J. *History of Hampstead.*
Pavitt, W. T. and K. *The Book of Talismans* (Rider, 1914).
Penrose, Alexander P. D. (ed.). *The Autobiography and Memoirs of Benjamin Robert Haydon* (Bell, 1927).
Picciotto. *Sketches of Anglo-Jewish History* (Trubner, 1875).
Potter, G. W. *Random Recollections of Hampstead* (Eyre & Spottiswoode, 1907).
Preston, J. H. *The Story of Hampstead* (Staples, 1948).
Proctor, Bryan Waller (Barry Cornwall). *An Autobiographical Fragment and Biographical Notes* (Bell, 1877).

Rollins, Hyder Edward (ed.). *The Keats Circle: Letters and Papers, 1816-1878* (Harvard, 1948).

Rollins, Hyder Edward (ed.); and Stephen Maxwell Parrish. *Keats and the Bostonians* (Harvard, 1951).

Rossetti, W. M. *Life of John Keats* ("Great Writers" Series. London. Walter Scott, 1887).

*Royal Academy Exhibitors, 1769-1904* (Henry Graves and George Bell, 1906).

Scott, Sir Walter, *The Fortunes of Nigel.*

Severn, Joseph. *Letters to H. Buxton Forman* (Oxford. Printed for private circulation, 1933).

Sharp, William. *Life and Letters of Joseph Severn* (Sampson Low, Marston & Co., 1892).

Sotheby, Wilkinson and Hodge. *Catalogue of the Original Love Letters of John Keats to Miss Fanny Brawne* (1885).

*Smits, ouden Heer: Kompleete Werken van den* (1877).

Speed, John Gilmer. Memoir in *The Poems of John Keats* (New York, Dodd Mead, 1883).

Spurgeon, Caroline. *Keats's Shakespeare* (O.U.P., 1928).

Strickland, W. G. *A Dictionary of Irish Artists* (Maunsel, 1913).

Swinburne, A. C. *Letters*, ed. Gosse and Wise (Heinemann, 1918).

Swinburne, A. C. *Miscellanies* (Chatto & Windus, 1886).

Tuckwell, Gertrude M., and Gwynn, Stephen. *The Life of the Rt. Hon. Sir Charles Wentworth Dilke, Bart., M.P.* (Murray, 1917).

Vernon (Joseph). *The New London and Country Songster* (1780 (?)).

Victoria County History: *Warwick*, vol. III (Oxford, 1945).

Walthamstow Antiquarian Society. *Some Walthamstow Houses* (Official Publication No. 12, 1924).

White, Caroline A. *Sweet Hampstead and its Associations* (Elliot Stock, 1900).

Williamson, George C. *The Keats Letters, Papers and Other Relics Forming the Dilke Bequest in the Hampstead Public Libraries* (John Lane, 1914).

# Index